In pra

'Thank you so much Gina Ford. You and your books are truly heaven sent.'

'Without your books I do not know what I would have done. Your advice has meant that I have a fantastic, happy little boy and I actually look forward to the next challenge he may bring as I know where the answer to any problem lies!'

'Gina transformed our son into the happiest, "easiest" baby that we could have wished for. Her knowledge and professionalism is astounding; she has answers to every question – and they really work.'

'From day one of Daisy's return home from hospital we put her into Gina's routine and have never looked back. Everyone comments on Daisy and what an unbelievably happy and contented baby she is . . . Thank you Gina for your books and the enjoyment and confidence they have given us.'

'Gina Ford worked for me as a maternity nurse. She is one of the rare people who has a natural understanding of and affinity with babies, combined with a sound theoretical grasp of sleep patterns and feeding requirements, based on extensive experience.'

'Gina Ford is rightly regarded as one of the top, most experienced maternity nurses in the UK. She sets very high standards for herself and for her mothers, and meets them. She is very loving with her babies, recognises and understands their changing needs and moods and ensures that they are entirely well cared for.'

'We can't recommend her highly enough to any prospective parents. We found her invaluable, and I have much to thank her for – setting us on the right path to understanding our baby's needs and being confident parents, as well as giving our son the best start in life he could get.'

The Contented Little Baby Book of Weaning

Your one-stop guide to contented feeding

Gina Ford

Vermilion

LONDON

3 5 7 9 10 8 6 4 2

First published in the United Kingdom in 2002 by Vermilion

This edition published in the United Kingdom in 2006
by Vermilion, an imprint of Ebury Publishing
Random House UK Ltd.
Random House
20 Vauxhall Bridge Road
London SW1V 2SA

Random House Australia (Pty) Limited
20 Alfred Street, Milsons Point, Sydney,
New South Wales 2061, Australia

Random House New Zealand Limited
18 Poland Road, Glenfield,
Auckland 10, New Zealand

Random House (Pty) Limited
Isle of Houghton, Corner Boundary Road & Carse O'Gowrie,
Houghton, 2198 South Africa

Random House UK Limited Reg. No. 954009
www.randomhouse.co.uk
Papers used by Vermilion are natural, recyclable products made from
wood grown in sustainable forests.

A CIP catalogue record is available for this book from the British Library.

ISBN: 0091912687
ISBN: 9780091912680 (from Jan 2007)

Printed and bound in Great Britain by Clays of St Ives plc

Please note that conversions to imperial weights and measures are suitable equivalents and not exact.

The information given in this book should not be treated as a substitute for qualified medical advice; always consult a medical practitioner. Neither the author nor the publisher can be held responsible for any loss or claim arising out of the use, or misuse, of the suggestions made or the failure to take medical advice.

Contents

For my god-daughter Brontë Sherbourne,
a very special and contented baby.

Acknowledgements

I would like to express my thanks and gratitude to the hundreds of parents whom I have worked with or advised over the years. Their constant feedback on their children's eating habits has been an enormous help in writing this book. In particular I would like to say a special thank you to Françoise and Steven Skelly – parents of Isabella and Oliver; Helen and David Sherbourne – parents of Alexander and Poppy; and Julie and Alvin Stardust – parents of Milly.

A special thank you to my Aunt Jean and Uncle Dan, and my cousins Ann Clough, Helen Ramsay and Sheila Eskdale for your love, continued support and encouragement and for helping look after my darling Molly. I would also like to thank my dear friends Jane Revell and Carla Fodden Flint for their special friendship and emotional support.

A very special debt of thanks to my agent, Emma Todd, my publisher, Fiona MacIntyre, and editors, Imogen Fortes and Miren Lopategui, and everyone else at Random House. I shall be eternally grateful for your never-ending support and endless patience.

My thanks, too, to Sara Lewis and Emma-Lee Gow for their help with compiling the recipes and to Paul Sacher, specialist clinical dietician, for his valuable contributions to the book. Becky Bagnell and Dawn Fozard also deserve a huge thank you for helping me with the manuscript.

And, finally, I am ever grateful for the huge support I receive from the thousands of readers of my books who take the time to contact me – a huge thank you to you all and much love to your contented babies.

Introduction

To establish long-term healthy eating habits for your baby you will need to put a lot of thought into the early stages of weaning – not only into the types of food you introduce, but also at which age they are introduced.

In my first weaning book nearly four years ago I claimed that a great many feeding diffculties stemmed from the lack of structure of milk feeding in the early days, leading to parents introducing solids too early, decreasing their baby's milk intake too rapidly thereby depriving him of the vital nutrients offered by milk. Another problem I used to encounter frequently was babies being introduced to solids too late. This results in the baby drinking vast amounts of milk and refusing solids long past a time when it is essential he is taking them.

The Department of Health in the UK now advises that babies should be exclusively breast-fed for the first six months of life. Between six and nine months, it is recommended that babies are introduced to a variety of different foods, gradually reducing the amount of milk they take and establishing them on three meals a day.

By one year, the theory is that a baby should be eating much the same food as the rest of the family. Sadly, however, for a large number of parents this is not the case and a great many find that by the time their baby reaches toddlerhood, mealtimes have become a battlefield involving much cajoling, tears and tantrums as worried parents try to persuade their children to eat small amounts of healthy foods. Evidence of this can be seen regularly on our screens via the many parenting programmes that highlight these problems or in newspapers and magazines which report that our childrens' diet is worse now than it was in the 1950's and a large number of teenagers are facing many serious health issues as a result of unhealthy eating habits in early life.

The feedback I have had over the years via my consultancy service and website www.contentedbaby.com is that the Contented Little Baby weaning plan has worked for thousands of babies around the globe. In this revised edition I have devised a new plan that fits in with the current recommendations to wean at six months. I realise, however, that all babies are individuals and in certain circumstances some parents are advised by their health visitor or GP to wean earlier than this. To ensure that milk remains the most important source of food for your baby, I have included a plan that gives step-by-step details of which are the best foods to introduce and at what time, so that the milk intake is not reduced too rapidly.

The book takes you through the different stages of weaning showing you what to do at each one. It also provides you with feeding plans and recipes for your baby and will help you avoid some of the common problems that many parents face during the first year.

The CLB feeding plans have worked for thousands of parents, resulting in a contented baby who eats a healthy, varied diet – they can work for your baby too.

Gina Ford

When to wean 1

The latest Department of Health (DoH) guidelines were published in 2003 and were prompted by recommendations from the World Health Organisation. They advise exclusive breast-feeding for the first six months of a baby's life, i.e. no solids or infant formula. The previous DoH advice was to wean between four and six months and not to give solids to any baby before four months (17 weeks). This is because it takes up to four months for the lining of a baby's gut to develop and for the kidneys to develop. Introducing solids too early can put a strain on the immature gut and kidneys, and many experts now believe that introducing solids before the baby's digestive system is ready to cope is the cause of the rapid increase in allergies over the last 20 years.

The advice in this latest edition of my weaning book is based on the recommendations of the DoH, and my personal experience of working with hundreds of babies plus the huge feedback that I have received from parents.

Up until 2003 when parents followed the previous DoH advice to wean between four and six months, I found that when a baby was ready to wean depended considerably on each individual baby. Because all babies are different and grow and develop at different rates, some needed weaning at four months, others would be nearer five months and some would manage to get to six months.

Weaning too early, increasing the amount of food too quickly or introducing the wrong types of food could result in some, if not all, of the following:

- Possible damage to the baby's digestive system. It takes up to four months for the lining of a baby's gut to develop and for the kidneys to mature enough to cope with the waste products from solid food. Introducing solids before your baby has a complete set of enzymes required to digest food properly could put pressure on his liver and kidneys and impair his digestive system.

- Physical problems when feeding. It is important not to start weaning before your baby's neuromuscular co-ordination has developed enough for him to control his head and neck while sitting upright supported in a chair to be fed. He should also be able to swallow food easily by moving it from the front of his mouth to the back. He will only be able to do this if he is supported upright.

- Introducing solids too early can put your baby at a higher risk of developing allergic conditions such asthma, eczema and hay fever.

- Scientific studies in Scotland found that a persistent cough was more common in babies who had been given solids before 12 weeks.

- A baby who is given solids too soon or increases them too rapidly may cut back too much on his milk and be denied the essential nutrients that milk provides.

- Early weaning can sometimes lead to overfeeding, making the baby overweight, which, research suggests, can lead to obesity in later life and increase the risk of cancer, diabetes, heart disease, etc.

While writing the latest edition of this book, I have spoken to many health professionals as well as hundreds of mothers via my website. It is clear that there is some controversy and confusion surrounding the latest government recommendations. Certainly, there are health professionals who believe that it is not weaning before four and six months that threatens a baby's health, but the kind of food the baby is given. It is also clear that there are some babies who seem not to be satisfied on milk alone for the full six months, and parents are struggling to cope with a miserable, fretful baby as they try to push him to six months on milk alone.

In this latest edition I give very detailed advice, which I hope will help you to get your baby happily to six months without introduction of solid foods. However, because I do not know your baby personally it is vital that you discuss with your health visitor or GP any concerns that you have about your baby showing signs that, despite reintroducing the extra feeds that I recommend, he is not being satisfied on milk alone.

The following guidelines should help you identify possible signs of your baby being ready to wean. Your baby could be ready if:

- He has been taking a full feed 4–5 times a day from both breasts or a 240ml (8oz) formula feed and has been happily going four hours from the beginning of one feed to the beginning of the next feed, but now gets irritable and chews his hands long before his next feed is due.

- He has been taking a full feed from both breasts or a 240ml (8oz) formula feed and screams for more when the feed finishes.

- He usually sleeps well at night, but starts to wake up earlier or in the middle of the night despite taking a full feed at 10/10.30pm. Daytime sleep becomes more erratic, waking up midway through a nap and not settling back or waking up earlier from naps.

- He is at least four months (17 weeks) old, has doubled his birth weight and weighs over 6.8kg (15lb), and your health visitor is happy with his weight gain each week.

If your baby is at least four months and showing most of these signs, despite having 4–5 full feeds a day, it could be that he is ready for weaning. If your baby is under six months you should tell your health visitor or GP so they can help you decide whether to proceed with the introduction of solids.

If you agree that your baby should wait until six months before having solids introduced, it is important that his increased hunger is met by introducing further milk feeds. Babies who have been sleeping through the night with only a small feed, and are waking earlier, should have the 10/10.30pm feed increased. Babies who are taking a full feed at 10/10.30pm and waking in the middle of the night may need to have a small milk feed in the middle of the night to get them through until 7am.

It is very important to remember that as your baby grows, so will his appetite. It is unreasonable to expect him to manage on only four milk feeds a day, when he is showing signs of increased hunger. Therefore, even if you have dropped the fifth feed you will probably need to reintroduce it until he starts weaning at six months.

Breast-fed babies

With babies who are being fully breast-fed it is more difficult to tell how much milk they are receiving. If your baby is over four months and showing most of the signs, you will need to talk in depth to your health visitor or GP about the choices available to you.

If he is under four months and not gaining enough weight each week, it is possible that your milk supply is getting very low in the evening. All that may be needed is extra milk, and I would advise that you follow my plan to increase your milk supply as laid out in *The New Contented Little Baby Book*. The extra milk that you express can be given to him as a top-up feed when your milk is at its lowest – usually in the evening, or it can be used to replace the 10/10.30pm feed, if your baby is waking up more than once in the night. Encourage your partner to do this feed so that you can get to bed early, after expressing whatever milk you have at 9/9.30pm, to avoid your milk supply dropping even further.

If you find that you are only producing 90–120ml (3–4oz) at this time, which would be much less than your baby may need to feed, you will need to add milk that you have expressed earlier in the day to make the feed up to the amount that your baby needs.

If you do not have an expressing machine and your baby refuses to take a bottle, you would need to put your baby to the breast more often to increase your milk supply and help satisfy his appetite. I would advise that you feed your baby at 7am and 10am, and then top-up prior to his lunchtime nap with a further breast-feed. Then feed him at 2/2.30pm and re-introduce the 5pm feed. This will give him an extra two feeds a day. I would also advise that you try to get a short rest after dinner in the evening, and delay the 10/10.30pm feed to 11pm to try and increase the amount he is getting at that feed.

I hope that the above suggestions help with increasing your milk supply and satisfying your baby's hunger. However, if your baby is still unsettled between feeds and his weight gain has not improved you should discuss with your health visitor about giving one complementary bottle of formula a day, preferably at the 10/10.30pm feed. By giving a full formula feed at this time, and expressing at 9.30pm, you can then use the milk that you expressed as a top-up during the day, thus avoiding further complementary feeding.

Early weaning

If your baby is over 17 weeks and having 5–6 full milk feeds, and still not managing to go happily between feeds, it is possible that he may need to be weaned early. Check the signs mentioned earlier that indicate that your baby is no longer satisfied by milk alone. I would then suggest that you keep a feeding and sleeping diary for 3–4 days to show to your health visitor or doctor so they can help you decide whether your baby should be weaned early. If they do advise that you should introduce solids before the recommended age of six months it is important to remember that milk is still the most important food, as it provides your baby with the right balance of vitamins and minerals. Solids given during early weaning should be classed as fillers, which should be increased very slowly over several weeks, gradually preparing your baby for three meals a day between six and seven months. By always offering the milk first, you will ensure that his daily milk intake does not decrease too rapidly if you have been advised to wean early.

It is also very important if you are weaning early to ensure that the foods you offer your baby are all from the first stage baby foods (see page 15), and that you do not start to introduce foods too early which could put your baby at risk of allergies.

Which foods?

During the first year babies grow rapidly, and most will have tripled their birth weight by the time they reach their first birthday. To ensure that your baby grows at the right rate, develops strong bones and teeth, firm muscles and healthy tissues it is essential that the food you give him has the right balance of nutrients. The following section divides food into the five different food groups. By giving your baby the recommended daily number of servings from each group shown, you can be sure that his daily nutritional needs are being met. For more information about creating a healthy, balanced diet for children see *The Contented Child's Food Bible*.

FOOD GROUPS FOR A NUTRITIONALLY ADEQUATE DIET

Group One: Milk, Dairy Products and Substitutes

Breast milk, infant formula, cow's milk, lassi, yoghurt, fromage frais, cottage cheese, hard cheese, infant soya formula, tofu.

Major nutrients
Energy (calories) and fat. Protein, calcium, vitamin A, B vitamins, zinc. Iron and vitamin D in breast and formula milks.

Milk will be your baby's main source of nutrition for the first six months of his life. Milk, dairy products or their substitutes remain a vital part of everyone's diet because they are a source of energy and contain some essential vitamins and minerals. In particular, calcium is necessary for the development and maintenance of healthy bones and teeth. It also ensures the muscles and nerves work properly. Vitamin A is important for growth and development as well as eyesight. Zinc helps with tissue growth and repair while vitamin B_{12} is vital for healthy blood cells and nerve function.

Group Two: Carbohydrates

Bread, rolls, baby cereals, fortified breakfast cereals, oats and other cereals, plain and savoury biscuits, potatoes, yams, millet, pasta, semolina, rice.

Major nutrients

Energy (calories). Thiamine, niacin, folic acid, vitamin B_6, biotin, zinc, fibre.

Carbohydrate supplies energy, the fuel for the body, which all children need to perform well and enjoy life. The B vitamins found in carbohydrates help the body to use this energy efficiently. Folic acid is vital for healthy blood cells. Fibre is found in unrefined carbohydrates and is important for a healthy digestive system. For more information about the different types of carbohydrate see *The Contented Child's Food Bible*.

Group Three: Vegetables and Fruit

Leafy and green vegetables (cabbage, green beans, peas, broccoli, leeks); root vegetables (carrots, onions, turnips); salad vegetables (tomatoes, cucumber), mushrooms, sweetcorn, marrow; fruit (apples, bananas, peaches, oranges, melons), fruit juices.

Major nutrients
Vitamins A, C and folic acid, fibre plus a host of other health-giving nutrients, e.g. trace elements and minerals, many of which function as antioxidants.

The antioxidants found in this food group help to protect the body from infection and disease. Vitamin C helps keep skin and tissue healthy and aids the absorption of iron. It also helps white blood cells to do their job of fighting infection. Fibre is vital for good digestion and maintaining a healthy gut.

Group Four: Meat and Meat Alternatives

Meat, poultry, eggs, fish, lentils, beans, baked beans.

Major nutrients
Energy (calories) and fat. Protein, iron, zinc, B vitamins (B_{12} in animal foods only).

Protein plays an essential role in building and repairing the body. It builds strong muscles and heart. The B vitamins help the body to use energy. Iron is vital for the production of healthy red blood cells. Essential fatty acids found in fat are essential for a strong immune system. They keep the skin and joints healthy and regulate hormones. Some types of fatty acid play a vital role in the development of the brain and eyesight.

Group Five: Occasional Foods

Cakes, sweet biscuits, sweetened squash, sweetened desserts and milk drinks, ice cream, cream, sugar, jam, honey, crisps, savoury snacks, fried and fatty foods.

These foods have little or no nutritional value. *None* of these foods is necessary in your baby's diet. They contain a lot of fat, energy, sugar or salt. Try not to use foods from this group every day.

Organic food

A report issued by the Soil Association in 2001 claimed that organic food is healthier for us because it contains more properties that help protect the body against cell damage and cancer. The report also claimed that organic food has improved levels of minerals and vitamin C.

This report, along with an increasing amount of other research into the benefits of organic food has seen the sale of organic food grow at an average rate of 40 per cent a year since 1995. Despite its increased popularity, however, organic food is still considerably more expensive than the non-organic option, which I'm sure plays a big part in people's choice on whether to go organic or not.

Although the government claims that permitted levels of pesticides used on non-organic crops pose no danger to our health, many scientists and food experts believe that even small amounts of these pesticide residues found in food can be harmful.

My own personal belief is that organic food is not only healthier for us, but it also tastes better. When it comes to babies and young children I believe passionately that it is our duty to give them the purest and best food available, particularly during the first two years of life when the building of their immune system is so dependent upon the food they eat.

I appreciate the extra cost involved for families on a budget but, in my opinion, if a choice has to be made on where to cut back on costs, it should never be on food. A child will not suffer long term from having fewer toys or wearing hand-me-down clothes, but a diet of food grown or reared using artificial fertilisers, pesticides, antibiotics and hormones could affect his immune system for life.

The following information should be helpful when considering whether or not to try and wean your baby on organic food:

- Organic food has to meet a strict set of standards regulated by EU law and governed in the UK by the UK Register of Organic Food Standards (UKROFS). Producers and manufacturers have to keep strict details of production, ingredients, distribution, etc., and all organic food is traceable back to its source.

- Organic fruit and vegetable producers are not permitted to use artificial pesticides, fertilisers and fungicides when growing or storing crops. Research shows that non-organic food can have traces of all these chemicals that cannot be removed by washing.

- Organic farmers must feed their livestock a natural diet so that they grow at a natural pace. Growth promoters are prohibited, as is the routine use of antibiotics.

Commercial baby food

Over the years I have encountered considerable problems with babies who are weaned on commercial baby foods – their taste buds become so accustomed to the bland taste of these processed foods that once they are old enough to participate in family meals they simply refuse. Although the introduction of organic ranges by some manufacturers has brought about an improvement in commercial baby food, it is still no match for the distinct flavours and different textures of home-made food.

I also believe that commercially prepared foods, particularly second-stage meals in jars and tins, do not provide enough calories to sustain the rapid growth of young babies, as they are not as energy-dense as home-cooked meals. I have discovered a significant link between night-time waking and commercial baby food. Many babies who previously slept through the night from 2–3 months will start to wake up several times a night between six months and one year, but once I advise parents to change their baby's diet to a home-cooked one there is nearly always a huge improvement in the baby's sleeping patterns. Many nutritional experts claim that a baby whose diet consists solely of commercial food will not receive enough of the right calories for healthy growth, which would account for such babies waking up genuinely hungry. For example, a home-made recipe for cauliflower cheese contains cauliflower, flour, butter, milk and cheese. A commercially prepared jar of cauliflower cheese may also contain these ingredients, but in lower amounts, and in addition is more than likely to be bulked out with other fillers such as rice, potato and maltodextrin. (Maltodextrin is a sweet bulking agent, usually derived from potato, corn or rice and used to enhance the artificial flavours in many adult foods. It is also used in the gum on postage stamps and envelopes!) None of these bulking agents adds anything of note to commercial baby foods.

If you want to establish lifelong healthy eating habits for your baby, try to restrict the use of commercially prepared baby meals. The occasional use of organic commercial foods without additives and fillers in conjunction with a variety of home-cooked meals is not a problem, but a diet made up mainly of jars and packets may not only create a fussy feeder, but also cause sleeping problems.

The following guidelines will help you choose the best commercially prepared foods on the market.

- Always check the labels for the list of ingredients, which are listed in order of quantity, the largest quantity always coming first. Avoid anything containing preservatives, artificial colourings, sugar, or fillers such as maltodextrin or water. Watch out for hidden sugars such as fructose, dextrose or sucrose.

- Choose pure baby cereals that are free of sugar, starch and maltodextrin. For babies under six months, cereals should also be gluten-free and not contain ingredients such as eggs, citrus fruits or tomatoes, which can trigger allergies.

- Always check the safety button on the top of jars. If the button is raised or the lid can be removed, do not buy it. Never feed your baby food straight from the jar or can. Put the amount he needs into a bowl and the remainder into a separate dish and refrigerate. Carefully follow the manufacturer's guidelines for heating, serving and storing leftovers.

Foods to be avoided

During the first two years of your baby's life, certain foods are best used sparingly, or avoided altogether, as they may be harmful to your baby's health. The two worst culprits in this regard are sugar and salt.

Sugar

During the first year of weaning it is best to avoid adding sugar to any of your baby's food, as it may make him develop a taste for sweet things. A baby's appetite for savoury foods can be seriously affected if he is allowed lots of foods containing sugar or sugar substitutes. But when buying commercial foods these ingredients can be hard to avoid. A survey by the Consumer's Association magazine, *Which?*, tested 420 baby products and reported that 40 per cent contained sugar or fruit juice, or both. When choosing baby cereals or commercial foods check the labels carefully; sugar may be listed as dextrose, fructose, glucose or sucrose. Watch out, too, for syrup or concentrated fruit juice, which are also sometimes used as sweeteners.

Too much sugar in the diet may not only make your baby refuse savoury foods, but can also lead to serious problems such as tooth decay and obesity. Because sugar converts very quickly to energy, babies and children who have too much may become very hyperactive. Products such as baked beans, spaghetti hoops, cornflakes, fish fingers, jam, tomato ketchup, tinned soups and some yoghurts are just a few of the everyday foods that contain hidden sugars, so care should be taken that when your baby reaches toddlerhood, he does not eat these foods in excess. It is also important to check the labels of fruit juices and squashes.

Salt

Children under two years of age should not have salt added to their food – they get all the salt they need from natural sources such as vegetables. Adding salt to a young baby's food can be very dangerous as it can put a strain on his immature kidneys. Research also shows that children who develop a taste for salt early in life may be more prone to heart disease later. When your baby reaches the stage of joining in with family meals, it is important that you do not add salt to the food during cooking. Remove your baby's portion, then add salt for the rest of the family.

As with sugar, many processed foods and commercially prepared meals contain high levels of salt. It is important to check the labels on these foods carefully before giving them to your toddler.

Preparing and cooking food for your baby

Making your own food not only often works out cheaper, but, more importantly, will be of great nutritional benefit to your baby. And it needn't be fiddly or time-consuming if you make up large quantities at a time and store mini meals away in the freezer (pages 53–8). Keep sterilised feeding equipment, ice cube trays and freezerproof containers at the ready and follow the general instructions below.

Sterilised feeding equipment

All feeding equipment should be sterilised for the first six months and bottles and teats for as long as they are used. Sterilise ice cube trays or freezer containers by boiling them in a large saucepan of water for five minutes, or soaking them in sterilising solution for 30 minutes. Use a steam steriliser, if you have one, for small items such as spoons or serving bowls and follow timings recommended in the manufacturer's handbook. Wash cooking utensils as usual in a dishwasher, or rinse handwashed items with boiling water from the kettle.

Packing food for the freezer

- Make sure cooked puréed food is covered as quickly as possible and transfer it to the freezer as soon as it is cool enough.

- Never put warm food into a refrigerator or freezer.

- Check the temperature of your freezer on a freezer thermometer. It should read −18°C. If you don't already have a freezer thermometer they can be bought from good hardware shops or the cookware section in large department stores.

- If using an ice cube tray, fill with puréed food, open-freeze until solid, then pop the cubes out of the tray and into a sterilised plastic box. Non-sterilised items such as plastic bags can be used from six months. Seal well and freeze.

- Label items clearly, adding the date.

- Use food within six weeks.

- Never refreeze cooked food. Food can only be put back into the freezer if it was originally frozen raw then defrosted and cooked – a raw frozen chicken breast, defrosted, for example, can be frozen as a cooked casserole.

Defrosting tips

Defrost frozen (covered) food in the fridge overnight or leave at room temperature if you forget, transferring it to the fridge as soon as it has defrosted. Make sure it is covered at all times and stand it on a plate to catch any drips. Never speed up defrosting by putting food into warm or hot water. Always use defrosted food within 24 hours.

Reheating tips

- When batch cooking, take out a portion of food for your baby to use now and freeze the rest. Don't be tempted to reheat the entire mixture and then freeze what is left.

- If your baby has only eaten a tiny portion it can be tempting to reheat and serve the leftovers later. Please don't – babies are much more susceptible than adults to food poisoning so get in the habit of throwing leftovers away immediately.

- Reheat foods only once.

First stage weaning 2

I have always believed that the foods a baby is introduced to during the first stage of weaning help to lay the foundation for healthy eating habits for the rest of his life. Of course, the majority of babies and toddlers will go through fussy spells where they eat less or refuse certain foods. But in general I have found that, in the long term, introducing the right foods at the right age helps ensure that a child will eat a varied diet during the early years.

Since the changes in the recommended age for weaning, I have received thousands of emails and calls from worried parents about how to go about introducing solids. The most confusing aspect for the majority of parents is how, when trying to follow the advice to start weaning at six months, they can introduce such a wide variety of the recommended foods at six months. I am not surprised by this confusion, because it does seem rather daunting to be told that your baby should be exclusively breast-fed for six months, then at six months you should be introducing a wide variety of vegetables, fruit, carbohydrates in the form of cereal, pasta, bread, etc., dairy products in the form of yoghurt, cheese, butter, etc., and on top of all of this, protein foods in the form of chicken, fish and meat, etc.

Because there have been no clear guidelines, other than to introduce these foods from six months on, I have found that many parents have been introducing so many different foods at the same time, that their babies have ended up with severe stomach pains or constipation problems, and sometimes even both. While it is important that all of the foods are introduced from six months of age, it is vital that they are introduced in a way that does not affect or put strain on the baby's digestive system.

For example, one of the most common problems that I have encountered is that parents exclusively breast-feed for six months, then within a week or two of introducing their baby to different fruits and vegetables they suddenly start introducing harder-to-digest foods such as chicken, cheese and meat. While it is important that these foods are introduced between six and seven months, it is of no benefit to the baby to introduce them before he is used to digesting a reasonable amount of other solids. Overloading his digestive system could result in causing your baby a lot of pain.

In my first stage weaning plans I have ensured that the foods recommended by the DoH are introduced at the right age, and at the right times so that these problems can be avoided.

Because all babies are different it is important that you discuss with your health visitor if your baby is showing the signs of needing to be weaned. I have taken into consideration that some health visitors or doctors are recommending weaning earlier than six months, if they feel the individual baby's needs cannot be met by milk alone.

The following guidelines will help you establish the right foods at the right age for your baby. Once you have read the guidelines you can then use them alongside the weaning plan that is appropriate for your baby's age.

Weaning guidelines

- Introduce solids after the 11am feed. Prepare everything you need for giving the solids in advance: baby chair, two bibs, two spoons and a clean, fresh damp cloth.

- Start by offering your baby one teaspoonful of pure organic rice mixed to a very smooth consistency using either expressed milk, formula or cool, filtered freshly boiled water.

- Make sure the baby rice is cooled enough before feeding it to your baby. Use a shallow plastic spoon – never a metal one, which can be too sharp or get too hot.

• Some babies need help in learning how to feed from the spoon. By placing the spoon just far enough into his mouth, and bringing the spoon up and out against the roof of his mouth, his upper gums will take the food off, encouraging him to feed.

• Once your baby is established on baby rice at 11am and is tolerating it, give the rice after the 6pm feed instead. When giving solids at 6pm, give the baby most of his milk first, then offer the solids. With babies who are being weaned early you can offer them a teaspoon at first, and then increase the amount after he has taken it for three consecutive days. With babies who are being weaned from six months you can follow the lead of your baby and increase the amount sooner.

• Once he is taking two teaspoonfuls of baby rice mixed with milk or water after the 6pm feed, a small amount of pear purée (page 53) can be introduced after the 11am feed.

• If the baby tolerates the pear purée, transfer it to the 6pm feed. Mixing the purée with baby rice in the evening will make it more palatable and prevent the baby from getting constipated.

• Small amounts of various organic vegetables and fruit can now be introduced after the 11am feed. To prevent your baby from developing a sweet tooth, try to give more vegetables than fruit. At this stage, avoid strong-tasting ones like broccoli or spinach, but, rather, concentrate on the root vegetables listed in the feeding plan at 4–5 months (see page 19). These contain natural sugars: they will taste sweeter and blander and may prove more palatable to your baby.

• Introduce a new food every three or four days if your baby is on the early weaning plan. If your baby is being weaned at six months you can introduce foods from the first stage weaning foods much more quickly. Keep a diary so you can see how your baby reacts to each new food.

• Always be very positive and smile when offering new foods. If your baby spits a food out, it may not mean that he dislikes it. Remember, this is all very new to him and different foods will get different reactions. If he positively refuses a food, however, leave it and try again in a week.

• If you are weaning early always offer milk first at the 11am and 6pm feed, as this is still the most important food at this stage in nutritional terms. While appetites do vary, in my experience the majority of babies will be drinking 840–900ml (28–30oz) of formula a day, or 4–5 full breast-feeds.

• If you are weaning at six months you should go straight into the *tier method* of feeding at the 11am feed. This is when you offer the baby half the milk first. Then give him most of his solids. For the remainder of the meal alternate between the remaining milk and solids until it is all gone. Continue to offer most of his milk first at the 6pm feed.

Early weaning

If you have been advised that your baby is ready for weaning before the recommended age of six months it is important to remember that milk is still the most important food for him. It provides him with the right balance of vitamins and minerals. Solids given before six months are classed as first tastes and fillers which should be increased very slowly over several weeks, gradually preparing your baby for three solid meals a day. By offering the milk first you will ensure that his daily milk intake does not decrease too rapidly before he reaches six months. Depending how old your baby is when you first introduce solids, he will probably still need a late feed at 10pm until solids are well established. However, as he increases his solids he should automatically cut down on his 10pm feed and, provided he has been sleeping through for at least two weeks, you should be able to eliminate the last couple of ounces at that feed by the time he reaches six months and is established on three meals a day.

Feeding plan at four to five months

This plan should be used as a guide to introduce your baby to solids. However, all babies differ and have their own likes and dislikes, so don't feel anxious if your child doesn't fit in exactly with the plan.

Food to introduce

Pure organic baby rice, pear, apple, carrot, sweet potato, potatoes, green beans, courgettes and swede.

Note: A 'cube' is equivalent to approximately one level tablespoon.

Days 1–3

7/7.30am	Breast-feed or 180–240ml (6–8oz) of formula milk
11am	Breast-feed or 180–240ml (6–8oz) of formula milk 1 tsp of pure organic baby rice mixed with breast milk, formula or cool boiled water
2/2.30pm	Breast-feed or 150–210ml (5–7oz) of formula milk
6pm	Breast-feed or 180–240 (6–8oz) of formula milk
10pm	Breast-feed or 150–210ml (5–7oz) of formula milk (optional)

Days 4–6

7/7.30am	Breast-feed or 180–240ml (6–8oz) of formula milk
11am	Breast-feed or 180–240ml (6–8oz) of formula milk 1 cube of pear purée (page 53), optional
2/2.30pm	Breast-feed or 150–210ml (5–7oz) of formula milk
6pm	Breast-feed or 180–240 (6–8oz) of formula milk 1–2 tsp of baby rice mixed with breast milk, formula or cool, boiled water
10pm	Breast-feed or 150ml (5oz) of formula milk (optional)

Days 7–9

7/7.30am	Breast-feed or 180–240ml (6–8oz) of formula milk
11am	Breast-feed or 180–240ml (6–8oz) of formula milk 1 cube of carrot purée (page 54)
2/2.30pm	Breast-feed or 150–210ml (5–7oz) of formula milk
6pm	Breast-feed or 180–240ml (6–8oz) of formula milk 1–2 tsp of baby rice mixed with breast milk, formula or cool boiled water, plus 1 cube of pear purée
10pm	Breast-feed or 150ml (5oz) of formula milk (optional)

Days 10–12

7/7.30am	Breast-feed or 180–240ml (6–8oz) of formula milk
11am	Breast-feed or 180–240ml (6–8oz) of formula milk 1 cube of apple purée (page 54)
2/2.30pm	Breast-feed or 150–210ml (5–7oz) of formula milk
6pm	Breast-feed or 180–240ml (6–8oz) of formula milk 2–3 tsp of baby rice mixed with breast milk, formula or cool boiled water
10pm	Breast-feed or 150ml (5oz) of formula milk (optional)

Days 13–15

7/7.30am	Breast-feed or 180–240ml (6–8oz) of formula milk
11am	Breast-feed or 180–240ml (6–8oz) of formula milk 1 cube of sweet potato purée (page 55)
2/2.30pm	Breast-feed or 150–210ml (5–7oz) of formula milk
6pm	Breast-feed or 180–240ml (6–8oz) of formula milk 2–3 tsp of baby rice mixed with breast milk, formula or cool boiled water plus 1 cube of pear purée

10pm   Breast-feed or 100–150ml (3⅓–5oz) of formula milk
(optional)

Days 16–18

7/7.30am   Breast-feed or 180–240ml (6–8oz) of formula milk

11am   Breast-feed or 180–240ml (6–8oz) of formula milk
1 cube of sweet potato purée or 1–2 tsp baby rice
mixed with 1 cube of courgette purée (page 55)

2/2.30pm   Breast-feed or 150–210ml (5–7oz) of formula milk

6pm   Breast-feed or 180–240ml (6–8oz) of formula milk
3–4 tsp of baby rice mixed with breast milk, formula
or cool boiled water plus 1 cube of apple or pear
purée

10pm   Breast-feed or 100–120ml (3⅓ –4oz) of formula milk
(optional)

Days 19–21

7/7.30am   Breast-feed or 180–240ml (6–8oz) of formula milk

11am   Breast-feed or 180–240ml (6–8oz) of formula milk
1–2 cubes of sweet potato purée or 1–2 tsp baby
rice mixed with 1 cube of carrot purée

2/2.30pm   Breast-feed or 150–210ml (5–7oz) of formula milk

6pm   Breast-feed or 180–240ml (6–8oz) of formula milk
3–4 tsp of baby rice mixed with breast milk, formula
or cool boiled water plus 1 cube of apple or pear
purée

10pm   Breast-feed or 60–90ml (2–3oz) of formula milk
(optional)

Days 22–24

7/7.30am   Breast-feed or 180–240ml (6–8oz) of formula milk

11am	Breast-feed or 180–240ml (6–8oz) of formula milk 1 cube of swede purée (page 56) mixed with either 2 cubes of sweet potato purée or 1–2 tsp baby rice
2/2.30pm	Breast-feed or 150–210ml (5–7oz) of formula milk
6pm	Breast-feed or 180–240ml (6–8oz) of formula milk 4–5 tsp of baby rice mixed with breast milk, formula or cool boiled water plus 1 cube of apple or pear purée
10pm	Breast-feed or 60–90ml (2–3oz) of formula milk (optional)

Days 25–27

7/7.30am	Breast-feed or 180–240ml (6–8oz) of formula milk
11am	Breast-feed or 180–240ml (6–8oz) of formula milk 1 cube of green bean purée (page 56) mixed with either 2 cubes of sweet potato purée or 2 tsp of baby rice
2/2.30pm	Breast-feed or 150–210ml (5–7oz) of formula milk
6pm	Breast-feed or 180–240ml (6–8oz) of formula milk 4 tsp of baby rice mixed with breast milk, formula or cool boiled water plus 2 cubes of apple purée
10pm	Breast-feed or 60ml (2oz) of formula milk (optional)

Days 28–30

7/7.30am	Breast-feed or 180–240ml (6–8oz) of formula milk
11am	Breast-feed or 180–240ml (6–8oz) of formula milk 1 cube of swede purée mixed with either 2 cubes of carrot purée or 2 tsp baby rice
2/2.30pm	Breast-feed or 150–210ml (5–7oz) of formula milk
6pm	Breast-feed or 180–240ml (6–8oz) of formula milk 4–5 tsp of baby rice mixed with breast milk, formula or cool boiled water plus 2 cubes of apple or pear purée

10pm   Breast-feed or 60ml (2oz) of formula milk (optional)
Note: By now your baby should be ready to drop this feed.

Five to six months

Babies who started weaning at the age of four months on medical advice, should have tasted baby rice, plus a variety of different vegetables and fruit. Most will by now be happy to take a combination of two or three different vegetables at lunchtime.

Somewhere between the ages of five and six months your baby will probably show signs of hunger long before his 11am feed is due. This is a sign that he is ready to start having breakfast, and a small amount of fruit purée can be introduced after his 7am milk feed.

If you start weaning at five months, work through the plan above faster than the given times. You should move on to the 5–6 month feeding plan below once your baby is used to all the foods above.

Feeding plan at five to six months

The following feeding plan is intended as a guide, so don't feel anxious if your baby seems to want a little more or less than the recommended serving.

Food to introduce

Oats, parsnips, mango, peaches, broccoli, avocados, peas and cauliflower.

Days 1–3

7am   Breast-feed or 180–240ml (6–8oz) of formula milk
1 tbsp of fruit purée (optional)

11am   Breast-feed or 150–210ml (5–7oz) of formula milk
4 cubes of sweet potato, carrot or courgette purée mashed together

2/2.30pm	Breast-feed or 150–210ml (5–7oz) of formula milk
6pm	Breast-feed or 180–240ml (6–8oz) of formula milk 4 tsp of baby rice mixed with breast milk, formula milk or cool boiled water plus 2 cubes of apple purée

Days 4–6

7am	Breast-feed or 180–240ml (6–8oz) of formula milk 1 tbsp of fruit purée (optional)
11am	Breast-feed or 150–180ml (5–6oz) of formula milk 4–5 cubes of sweet potato, swede and green bean purée mashed together
2/2.30pm	Breast-feed or 150–210ml (5–7oz) of formula milk
6pm	Breast-feed or 180–240ml (6–8oz) of formula milk 4 tsp of baby rice mixed with breast milk, formula milk or cool boiled water plus 2 cubes of apple or pear purée

Days 7–9

7am	Breast-feed or 180–240ml (6–8oz) of formula milk 1–2 cubes of fruit purée
11am	Breast-feed or 150–180ml (5–6oz) of formula milk 2 tbsp of mashed avocado mixed with 2 cubes of apple purée
2/2.30pm	Breast-feed or 150–210ml (5–7oz) of formula milk
6pm	Breast-feed or 180–240ml (6–8oz) of formula milk 4–5 tsp of baby rice mixed with breast milk or formula, plus 2 cubes of apple, peach or pear purée

Days 10–12

7am	Breast-feed or 180–240ml (6–8oz) of formula milk 1–2 cubes of fruit purée

11am Breast-feed or 120–150ml (4–5oz) of formula milk
3 cubes of sweet potato purée mixed with 2 cubes of
courgette or carrot purée

2/2.30pm Breast-feed or 150–210ml (5–7oz) of formula milk

6pm Breast-feed or 180–240ml (6–8oz) of formula milk
4–5 tsp of baby rice mixed with breast milk or
formula, plus 2 cubes of apple, pear or peach purée

Days 13–15

7am Breast-feed or 180–240ml (6–8oz) of formula milk
1–2 cubes of fruit purée

11am Breast-feed or 120–150ml (4–5oz) of formula milk
2 cubes of sweet potato purée mixed with 1 cube of
carrot purée and 1 cube of courgette purée

2/2.30pm Breast-feed or 150–210ml (5–7oz) of formula milk

6pm Breast-feed or 180–240ml (6–8oz) of formula milk
5–6 tsp of baby rice mixed with breast milk or
formula, plus 2 cubes of apple, pear or peach purée

Days 16–18

7am Breast-feed or 180–240ml (6–8oz) of formula milk
2–3 cubes of fruit purée

11.30am Breast-feed or 90–120ml (3–4oz) of formula milk
2 cubes of sweet potato purée mixed with 2 cubes of
carrot purée, 1 cube of sweet potato and 1 tbsp of
home–made chicken stock (page 58)

2/2.30pm Breast-feed or 150–210ml (5–7oz) of formula milk

6pm Breast-feed or 180–240ml (6–8oz) of formula milk
4–5 tsp of baby rice mixed with breast milk or
formula, plus 2 cubes of apple, pear or peach
purée

Days 19–21

7/7.30am   Breast-feed or 180–240ml (6–8oz) of formula milk
2–3 cubes of fruit purée

11.30am   Breast-feed or 90ml (3oz) of formula milk
3 cubes of sweet potato purée mixed with 2 cubes of
cauliflower purée (page 57)

2/2.30pm   Breast-feed or 150–210ml (5–7oz) of formula milk

6pm   Breast-feed or 180–240ml (6–8oz) of formula milk
5–6 tsp of baby rice mixed with breast milk, formula
milk or cool boiled water, plus 2 cubes of apple,
pear or peach purée

Days 22–24

7/7.30am   Breast-feed or 180–240ml (6–8oz) of formula milk
1 tsp of oat cereal mixed with breast milk or
formula plus 2 cubes of apple, pear or peach purée

11.45am   Breast-feed or 90–120ml (3–4oz) of formula milk
3 cubes of sweet potato purée mixed with 2 cubes of
broccoli purée (page 58)

2/2.30pm   Breast-feed or 150–210ml (5–7oz) of formula milk

6pm   Breast-feed or 180–240ml (6–8oz) of formula milk
5–6 tsp of baby rice mixed with breast milk or
formula, plus 2 cubes of apple, pear or peach purée

Days 25–27

7/7.30am   Breast-feed or 180–240ml (6–8oz) of formula milk
1 tsp of oat cereal mixed with breast milk or
formula mixed with half a mashed banana

11.45am   Breast-feed or 90–120ml (3–4oz) of formula milk
3 cubes of sweet potato purée mixed with 2 cubes of
carrot purée, plus 1 cube of cauliflower purée

2/2.30pm	Breast-feed or 150–210ml (5–7oz) of formula milk
6pm	Breast-feed or 180–240ml (6–8oz) of formula milk 5–6 tsp of baby rice mixed with breast milk, formula milk or cool boiled water, plus 2 cubes of apple, pear or peach purée

Days 28–30

7/7.30am	Breast-feed or 180–240ml (6–8oz) of formula milk 1–2 tsp of oat cereal mixed with breast milk or formula plus 2 cubes of apple, pear or peach purée
11.45am	Breast-feed or 90–120ml (3–4oz) of formula milk 2 cubes of sweet potato purée mixed with 2 cubes of parsnip purée, plus 2 cubes of broccoli purée
2/2.30pm	Breast-feed or 150–210ml (5–7oz) of formula milk
6pm	Breast-feed or 180–240ml (6–8oz) of formula milk 5–6 tsp of baby rice mixed with breast milk, formula milk or cool boiled water, plus 2 cubes of pear purée

Introducing protein

If your baby was introduced to solids before six months, by the time he reaches six months he should have tasted a wide variety of vegetables and fruit, and be used to digesting reasonable amounts of carbohydrate in the form of potato and baby rice. He will be ready for the introduction of protein between six and seven months.

When your baby reaches six months you can introduce chicken, fish, meat, pulses and dairy products. I would advise that you introduce these foods slowly during the early stages, introducing a new food every three days to ensure that your baby does not have a bad response to a particular food. Start by replacing two of his vegetable cubes with two cubes of the more simple chicken, fish, meat or pulse recipes. Increase the amount by one or two cubes a day until your baby's meal consists totally of one of the protein recipes.

It is very easy to get into the habit of serving the same favourite foods to your baby, but this could lead to him becoming very fussy about the foods he eats. I therefore advise that once your baby is established on the different protein meals, you should use the feeding plans as a guide to ensure that your baby receives a variety of different foods and meals each week.

Once a protein is established at lunchtime, the rice and fruit in the evening can gradually be replaced with other savoury foods. By the time your baby reaches seven months, his daily feeding plan should look similar to the feeding plans that follow. Parents and carers should use these plans as a guide; all babies differ, so don't feel anxious if your child doesn't appear to like a particular food or seems to want a little more or less. Be guided by your baby.

Weaning at six to seven months

The previous DoH advice was to wean between four and six months. It advised that new foods were introduced every 3–4 days. This was to reduce the risk of allergies, and avoid solids being increased too quickly, resulting in too rapid a decrease in the milk intake. Starting weaning at six months coincides with the age that a baby's natural store of iron, with which he is born, is getting very low. Therefore it is important that you progress through the first stage weaning foods (pages 19 and 23) much more quickly than previously recommended to ensure that your baby it introduced to iron-containing foods. The first recommended food to give is baby rice: choose one that is fortified with iron. Within a couple of days of introducing baby rice you should then progress quickly through the food groups to ensure that your baby is getting enough iron-rich foods. Introduce a new food every couple of days, and increase the amounts he is having every couple of days.

When starting weaning at six months you should also immediately go on to the tier system of feeding at lunchtime (see page 18), as this will encourage your baby to increase his solids more rapidly.

If you do not reduce your baby's milk intake at this feed you may find that he becomes very fussy about weaning, and rejects many of the foods you are introducing.

By seven months you should aim to have reduced your baby's milk intake to three milk feeds a day, and to have established him on a proper lunch and tea with a small breakfast. If your baby is fussy about solids but still taking 4–6 milk feeds a day, it is important that you reduce the milk that he is taking so as to improve his appetite for the solids.

The 10pm feed

Many babies continue to need a feed at 10pm to get them through the night until solids are well established. If your baby is following the Contented Little Baby (CLB) routines during the day and sleeping through from 11pm to 7am, with only a small feed at 10/10.30pm, then introducing solids and weaning him off this feed should be fairly simple. As the amount of solids he takes at teatime increases, then the amount he wants at the late feed should decrease. If he does not cut back automatically, as long as he is sleeping through to 7am I would suggest that you gradually reduce the amount he is taking. For breast-fed babies you can reduce the feed by a few minutes, and for formula-fed babies you should reduce the amount he takes by 30ml (1oz). Provided he sleeps through, you can continue to reduce this feed by those amounts every three nights. Once you reach a stage where he has slept through for several nights on a very short breast-feed of around five minutes or a formula-feed of a couple ounces, you should safely be able to cut the feed out altogether, without worrying about him waking up hungry earlier.

With babies who are taking a full breast-feed or formula-feed it could take at least 3–4 weeks to eliminate the late feed. There is no benefit to reducing it too quickly and having your baby waking up earlier. Many babies will take a full feed at 10pm, then wake up and only take a small milk feed at breakfast time – they then demand a big milk feed at 11am and refuse solids at this time. They then proceed to demand a further big feed at 2.30pm. When this situation occurs it can be very tempting just to cut out the 10pm feed altogether so that the baby wakes up and takes a full feed at 7am. However, this can lead to the problem of the baby waking up earlier, which in turn throws the whole day out. If you find your baby still needs a full feed at 10/10.30pm to get through the night, I would suggest that you continue with this, but look at his overall daily milk intake, to see where else in the day you can reduce his milk intake to make the introduction of solids easier, and to get him on to three full milk feeds between 7am and 7pm.

In my experience the simplest way to do this is to accept that, for a couple of weeks, your baby needs more at 10pm, but look to cut down the amount of milk he has at 11am and 2.30pm quite severely. This will encourage him to eat more solids after the 11am milk feed, and be more ready for solids in the evening. Once he starts to take a reasonable amount of solids at this time, you can then start to decrease the amount of milk he is taking at 10pm, using the method already described above. As this feed decreases, you should see an increase in the 7am milk feed. You should continue to decrease the 11am milk feed as suggested in the feeding plan, but once he is only taking a very small amount at this time, you would need to increase the 2/2.30pm milk feed, so that he is starting to take most of his daily intake between the 7am, 2/2.30pm and the 6.30pm feed.

Whilst doing it this way may take longer to eliminate the 10/10.30pm feed, it will ensure that you do not end up with your baby waking at 5am and genuinely needing to feed.

Once he is increasing the amount of solids he is taking during the day, and taking near enough the amounts of milk at the recommended times in the feeding plan you can then gradually start to reduce the amount of milk he is taking at 10pm using the method already described, without worrying about the risk of him waking earlier.

Introducing solids at 11am

Follow the suggested times for feeds, but instead of giving all of the milk first at the 11am feed it is important that you only give half of the milk, so that your baby is hungry enough to accept the solids. Continue to reduce the time he is on the breast before he has his solids by 2 to 3 minutes every couple of days. If your baby is formula-fed, then reduce his feed by 30g (1oz) every couple of days. Within 7–10 days you should have reached a stage where he is taking a very short breast-feed, or around 90ml (3oz) of formula, before his solids. You should still offer him a short breast-feed or a couple of ounces of milk after his solids. However, if he is looking for more milk, this is an indication that you need to increase more rapidly the amount of solids you are giving him.

Continue to decrease the milk he is taking at the 11am feed, until he is happy to start with his solids at lunchtime. Once he is taking 4–6 cubes he should have cut the amount of milk he is taking after the solids until he is only taking a few minutes on the breast or a couple of ounces of formula.

Once he reaches this stage you should then start to introduce small amounts of protein at lunchtime. Begin by replacing two of the vegetable cubes with two cubes of one of the simpler protein meals, such as chicken casserole, lentil casserole, etc. Continue to replace a cube of vegetables each day with a cube of the protein meal, until his lunch consists of a complete meal from one of the protein recipes. Once you reach this stage any top-up milk should be replaced with a drink of well-diluted juice or cool boiled water from a beaker (cup with lid).

Introducing solids in the evening

Within a couple of days of introducing baby rice at 11am, you should progress to introducing solids in the evening as well. For the first week I would advise that you give him the solids after he has taken most of his 6pm feed. This will encourage him to cut back on his 10pm feed, which will have a knock-on effect of him being hungrier for his first milk feed of the day. You should increase the amounts you give him, but do so on alternate days to the days on which you are increasing the lunchtime solids. Remember that the baby rice is far more filling than fruit, so increase that more rapidly than the fruit. Once your baby is taking nearer the quantities that I have mentioned in the feeding plan below, you should automatically see a decrease in his 10pm feed. If he does not cut back of his own accord, I would suggest that you reduce his 10pm feed gradually by 15g (½oz) every couple of nights provided, of course, that he continues to sleep through to 6/7am.

The following plan gives an example of how to introduce solids during the first week of weaning at six months. Please remember this is only an example; all babies are different so be guided by your baby's needs:

First week of weaning

Foods to choose during the first week of weaning are pure organic baby rice fortified with iron, pear, apple, carrot, sweet potato, swede, courgette.

Note: A 'cube' is a level tablespoon (15ml) or three teaspoonfuls.

Days 1–2

7/7.30am	Breast-feed or 180–240ml (6–8oz) of formula milk
11.00am	Breast-feed or 120–150ml (4–5oz) of formula milk 1–2 tsp of baby rice mixed with breast milk, formula or cool boiled water Small top-up of breast milk or formula milk
2/2.30pm	Breast-feed or 180–240ml (6–8oz) of formula milk
6pm	Breast-feed or 180–240ml (6–8oz) of formula milk
10pm	Breast-feed or formula-feed (optional)

Days 3–4

7/7.30am   Breast-feed or 180–240ml (6–8oz) of formula milk

11.00am   Breast-feed or 120–150ml (4–5oz) of formula milk
1 cube of fruit purée
Small top-up of breast milk or formula milk

2/2.30pm   Breast-feed or 180–240ml (6–8 oz) of formula milk

6pm   Breast-feed or 180–240ml (6–8oz) of formula milk
1–2 tsp of baby rice mixed with breast milk, formula
or cool boiled water
Remainder of milk feed

10pm   Breast-feed or formula-feed (optional)

Days 5–6

7/7.30am   Breast-feed or 180–240ml (6–8oz) of formula milk

11.00am   Breast-feed or 120–150ml (4–5oz) of formula milk
1–2 cubes of sweet potato purée
Small top-up of breast milk or formula milk

2/2.30pm   Breast-feed or 180–240 (6–8oz) of formula milk

6pm   Breast-feed or 180–240ml (6–8oz) of formula milk
2–3 tsp of baby rice mixed with breast milk, formula
or cool boiled water, mixed with 1 cube of fruit
purée
Remainder of milk feed

10pm   Breast-feed or formula-feed (optional)

Day 7

7/7.30am   Breast-feed or 180–240ml (6–8oz) of formula milk

11.00am   Breast-feed or 90–120ml (3–4oz) of formula milk
1 cube of vegetable purée mixed with either 1–2
cubes of sweet potato purée or 1–2 tsp of baby rice
Small top-up of breast milk or formula milk

2/2.30pm	Breast-feed or 180–240ml (6–8oz) of formula milk
6pm	Breast-feed or 180–240ml (6–8oz) of formula milk 3–4 tsp of baby rice mixed with breast milk, formula or cool boiled water, mixed with 1 cube of fruit purée
10pm	Breast-feed or formula-feed (optional)

Second week of weaning

During the second week of weaning, you should continue to introduce the foods suggested from the two lists of first stage weaning foods (see pages 19 and 23). You should aim to reduce the milk your baby is having before his solids at 11am. Breast-fed babies should gradually have the time they are on the breast reduced before being offered solids, and formula-fed babies should gradually have the amount of milk they are taking before solids reduced over the next seven days, until they are taking 90–120ml (3–4oz) before their solids. If you continue to allow your baby to take much more than this before his solids, you may find that he is not so interested in his solids or he may even refuse them altogether. It is important that he starts to increase the amount of solids at this age, so that you can progress quickly on to more iron-rich foods.

By day seven of this week you should have moved the evening solids forward to about 5.30pm, with half the milk before the solids, and the other half after the bath. By the end of the month you are working towards establishing breakfast, lunch and tea, and no milk feed at either lunchtime or teatime. Instead offer your baby a drink of cool boiled water or well-diluted juice from a beaker.

If your baby is still taking a full feed at 10/10.30pm and sleeping soundly to 7am, then I would reduce the amount he is taking at 10/10.30pm every three days. For breast-fed babies, reduce by five minutes on the breast, and formula-fed babies by 30ml (1oz) at a time.

Days 1–3

| **7/7.30am** | Breast-feed or 180–240ml (6–8oz) of formula milk |
| **11.00am** | Breast-feed or 90–120ml (3–4oz) of formula milk |

1–2 cubes of sweet potato purée or 1–2 tsp of baby rice mixed with two cubes of vegetable purée

2/2.30pm   Breast-feed or 180–240ml (6–8oz) of formula milk

6pm   Breast-feed or 180–240ml (6–8oz) of formula milk
3–4 tsp of baby rice mixed with breast milk, formula or cool boiled water, mixed with 1 cube of fruit purée

10pm   Breast-feed or formula feed (optional)

Days 4–7

7/7.30am   Breast-feed or 180–240ml (6–8oz) of formula milk

11.00am   Breast-feed or 90–120ml (3–4oz) of formula milk
2 cubes of sweet potato or 2 tsp of baby rice mixed with milk, plus 2–3 cubes of vegetable purée from the first stage weaning selection

2/2.30pm   Breast-feed or 180–240ml (6–8oz) of formula milk

5.30pm   Offer one breast or half the 180–240ml (6–8oz) of formula milk
4–5 tsp of baby rice mixed with breast milk, formula or cool boiled water, mixed with 1–2 cubes of fruit purée

6.30pm   After the bath offer the second breast or the remainder of the formula feed

Note: It is important to increase the ratio of baby rice much more quickly than the fruit purée, as the baby rice is much more filling.

10pm   Breast-feed or formula-feed (optional)

Third week of weaning

During the third week of weaning, you should continue to reduce the amount of milk your baby is having before his solids. Breast-fed babies should be taking no more than a few minutes before being offered solids and formula-fed babies should be taking between 60–90ml (2–3oz) before being offered solids. As the solids have increased, you should find that the top-up milk feed after the solids has reduced. Remember that by the end of six months you should, ideally, have eliminated the 11am milk feed altogether in order to encourage your baby towards a feeding plan of three solid meals a day and three milk feeds a day. Mixing small amounts of chicken stock with his vegetable purées will help prepare him for the different tastes of protein. Provided he is still sleeping through to nearer 7am, you should continue to reduce the 10pm feed gradually every couple of days.

Your baby should now be used to taking a variety of vegetables from the first stage weaning and you can begin to introduce him to stronger-tasting vegetables.

You will probably find that your baby will accept these vegetables more readily if you mix them with a ratio of three to one, of carbohydrates to vegetables, e.g. three cubes of sweet potato or three teaspoonfuls of baby rice to one cube of green beans or courgettes. Once he is happily taking this you can increase the cube of green vegetables by a further cube.

If you find that your baby is not managing to get to 11am and is looking for food before this time, I would suggest that now would be a good time to introduce a small amount of solids at breakfast. Starting him off with a small amount of yoghurt and fruit will prepare him for the introduction of cereal the following week.

Foods to introduce this week are broccoli, cauliflower, peas, peaches, mango, parsnips, avocado and yoghurt.

Days 1–3

7/7.30am   Breast-feed or 180–240ml (6–8oz) of formula milk
1–2 tbsp of yoghurt plus 1–2 cubes of fruit purée

11.00am   Breast-feed or 60–90ml (2–3oz) of formula milk
2–3 cubes of sweet potato plus 1 cube of vegetable purée from the first stage weaning selection mixed

with a little chicken stock

2/2.30pm   Breast-feed or 180–240ml (6–8oz) of formula milk

5.30pm   4–5 tsp of baby rice mixed with breast milk, formula
or cool boiled water, mixed with 2 cubes of fruit
purée

6.30pm   Breast-feed or 180–240ml (6–8oz) formula milk

10/10.30pm Breast-feed or formula-feed (optional)

Days 4–7

7/7.30am   Breast-feed or 180–240 ml (6–8oz) of formula milk
2–3 tbsp of oat cereal mixed with breast milk or
formula, plus 1–2 cubes of fruit purée

11.15/30am Breast-feed or 60–90ml (2–3oz) of formula milk
2–3 cubes of sweet potato and root vegetable purée
plus 1–2 cubes of cauliflower or green vegetable
purée from the second stage weaning selection
mixed with some chicken stock

2/2.30pm   Breast-feed or 180–240ml (6–8 oz) of formula milk

5pm   5–6 tsp of baby rice mixed with breast milk, formula
or cool boiled water, mixed with 2 cubes of
fruit/root vegetable purée

6.30pm   Breast-feed or 180–240ml (6–8oz) of formula milk

10pm   Breast-feed or formula-feed (optional)

Fourth week of weaning

During the fourth week of weaning, you should be preparing your
baby for the introduction of protein foods. Continue to introduce
the foods listed above, mixing small amounts of chicken stock with
his vegetable purées. Lentils and chicken are ideal forms of first
stage protein, but it is important that your baby is used to digesting
reasonable quantities of first stage foods before you introduce protein. Although all babies are different in the amounts they eat, I

have found that when babies are introduced to protein when they are taking only small amounts of vegetables, they do sometimes suffer from digestive problems. Ideally, your baby should be used to digesting around six ice cubes or six tablespoonfuls of mixed vegetables before you introduce animal protein or pulses at lunchtime. If you have already introduced a small amount of solids at breakfast, you can now begin to replace the yoghurt and fruit at breakfast with a small amount of oat cereal and fruit purée.

Day 1

7/7.30am   Breast-feed or 180–240ml (6–8oz) of formula milk
1–2 tbsp of oat cereal mixed with breast milk or formula, plus 2 cubes of fruit purée

11.30/45am 3–4 cubes of vegetable purée plus 2 cubes of chicken casserole purée (see page 85)
Drink of cool boiled water or well-diluted juice from a beaker

2/2.30pm   Breast-feed or 180–240ml (6–8oz) of formula milk

5pm   5–6 tsp of baby rice mixed with breast milk, formula or cool boiled water, plus 2 cubes of fruit or vegetable purée

6.30pm   Breast-feed or 180–240ml (6–8oz) of formula milk

10.30pm   Breast-feed or formula-feed (optional)

Day 2

7/7.30am   Breast-feed or 180–240ml (6–8oz) of formula milk
1–2 tbsp of oat cereal mixed with breast milk or formula, plus 2 cubes of fruit purée

11.30/45am 3 cubes of vegetable purée plus 3 cubes of chicken casserole purée
Drink of cool boiled water or well-diluted juice from a beaker

2/2.30pm	Breast-feed or 180–240ml (6–8oz) of formula milk
5pm	5–6 tsp of baby rice mixed with breast milk, formula or cool boiled water, plus 2 cubes of fruit or vegetable purée
6.30pm	Breast-feed or 180–240ml (6–8oz) of formula milk
10.30pm	Breast-feed or formula-feed (optional)

Day 3

7/7.30am	Breast-feed or 180–240ml (6–8oz) of formula milk 1–2 tbsp of oat cereal mixed with breast milk or formula, plus 2 cubes of fruit purée
11.30/45am	2 cubes of vegetable purée plus 4 cubes of chicken casserole purée Drink of cool boiled water or well-diluted juice from a beaker
2/2.30pm	Breast-feed or 180–240ml (6–8oz) of formula milk
5pm	5–6 tsp of baby rice mixed with breast milk, formula or cool boiled water, plus 2 cubes of fruit or vegetable purée
6.30pm	Breast-feed or 180–240ml (6–8oz) of formula milk
10.30pm	Breast-feed or formula-feed (optional)

Day 4

7/7.30am	Breast-feed or 180–240ml (6–8oz) of formula milk 1–2 tbsp of oat cereal mixed with breast milk or formula, plus 2 cubes of fruit purée
11.30/45am	4 cubes of vegetable purée plus 2 cubes of red lentil savoury purée (see page 89) Drink of cool boiled water or well-diluted juice from a beaker
2/2.30pm	Breast-feed or 180–240ml (6–8oz) of formula milk

5pm	5–6 tsp of baby rice mixed with breast milk, formula or cool boiled water, plus 2 cubes of fruit or vegetable purée
6.30pm	Breast-feed or 180–240ml (6–8oz) of formula milk
10.30pm	Breast-feed or formula-feed (optional)

Day 5

7/7.30am	Breast-feed or 180–240ml (6–8oz) of formula milk 1–2 tbsp of oat cereal mixed with breast milk or formula, plus 2 cubes of fruit purée
11.30/45am	3 cubes of vegetable purée plus 3 cubes of red lentil savoury purée Drink of cool boiled water or well-diluted juice from a beaker
2/2.30pm	Breast-feed or 180–240ml (6–8oz) of formula milk
5pm	5–6 tsp of baby rice mixed with breast milk, formula or cool boiled water, plus 2 cubes of fruit or vegetable purée
6.30pm	Breast-feed or 180–240ml (6–8oz) of formula milk
10.30pm	Breast-feed or formula-feed (optional)

Day 6

7/7.30am	Breast-feed or 180–240ml (6–8oz) of formula milk 1–2 tbsp of oat cereal mixed with breast milk or formula, plus 2 cubes of fruit purée
11.30/45am	2 cubes of vegetable purée plus 4 cubes of red lentil savoury purée Drink of cool boiled water or well-diluted juice from a beaker
2/2.30pm	Breast-feed or 180–240ml (6–8oz) of formula milk
5pm	5–6 tsp of baby rice mixed with breast milk, formula

or cool boiled water, plus 2 cubes of fruit or
vegetable purée

6.30pm   Breast-feed or 180–240ml (6–8oz) of formula milk

10.30pm   Breast-feed or formula-feed (optional)

Day 7

7/7.30am   Breast-feed or 180–240ml (6–8oz) of formula milk
1–2 tbsp of oat cereal mixed with breast milk or
formula, plus 2 cubes of fruit purée

11.30/45am 6 cubes of red lentil savoury or chicken casserole
purée
Drink of cool boiled water or well-diluted juice
from a beaker

2/2.30pm   Breast-feed or 180–240ml (6–8oz) of formula milk

5pm   5–6 tsp of baby rice mixed with breast milk, formula
or cool boiled water, plus 2 cubes of fruit or
vegetable purée

6.30pm   Breast-feed or 180–240ml (6–8oz) of formula milk

10.30pm   Breast-feed or formula-feed (optional)

Oliver: aged 5½ months

Oliver was introduced to a variety of fruits and vegetables between four and five months after his mother was advised to wean early. At five months he was cared for by the family's nanny for four days while his parents were on a business trip. During that time he suddenly started to get very fussy with his solids, eventually refusing the home-made vegetable purées. The nanny – anxious that he would go hungry – started giving him fruit purée at every meal. By the time his parents returned from their trip, Oliver would scream every time he was offered anything other than baby rice and fruit purée.

Feeding soon became a battle of wills as Oliver's mother tried to coax and cajole him into eating vegetables. She tried disguising the vegetables by mixing them with lots of fruit but Oliver still refused. After two weeks of battling and screaming at every meal she rang me for advice. As Oliver was under six months old, I advised his mother to take him right back to the very first stage of weaning. For three days, Oliver should be given baby rice mixed with milk and without fruit. On the fourth day I suggested that half a teaspoonful of puréed courgette should be mixed in with five teaspoonfuls of baby rice mixed with milk. Over the next few days Oliver's mother was to increase the courgette purée by no more than half a teaspoon each day. Once Oliver was taking two teaspoons of courgette purée with rice, I suggested that we try replacing the rice at lunchtime with sweet potato mixed with milk and courgette. Oliver happily took the sweet potato and the following day we introduced half a teaspoon of carrot with the sweet potato. Over the next couple of weeks we very slowly introduced different vegetables along with the sweet potato or baby rice, always starting off with no more than half a teaspoon, and always increasing it very slowly.

By the time Oliver was six and a half months old he was happily eating a wide range of vegetables at lunch and tea, plus chicken casserole or red lentil savoury. We did introduce fruit again but kept it to breakfast time until Oliver was seven months old. Obviously fruit plays an important part in a baby's diet but if your baby shows signs of developing a very sweet tooth, I would suggest that you restrict the amount you introduce until your baby is well established on vegetables.

When trying to solve a problem like Oliver's it is very important to take things very slowly and not increase the ratio of vegetables to baby rice too quickly. Until a baby reaches six months, milk still supplies the right balance of nutrients regardless of whether you are advised to wean your baby early.

Matthew: aged 5½ months

When Matthew was just over four months old his mother was advised to wean him early as he was showing all of the signs of needing solid food. She began to follow my guidelines. Matthew took to solids quickly and slept regularly from his last feed until 7am. Things went well for six weeks until one night Matthew suddenly woke up hungry at 2am. His mother was concerned that he might be genuinely hungry as he had only taken 150ml (5oz) at the 6pm feed, so she offered him a small 120ml (4oz) feed. Matthew drank this quickly but still refused to settle back to sleep until he was given a further 120ml (4oz) of formula. He then settled back to sleep very quickly and had to be woken at 7am.

During the following week Matthew became more and more difficult over his daytime milk feeds, and a pattern soon emerged of him taking only 120–150ml (4–5oz) at each of his daytime feeds, and only 90–120ml (3–4oz) at

6.15pm, before waking up desperately hungry between 2am and 3am. When his mother contacted me for advice she assured me she was following my routines and guidelines to the letter. The daily records she sent me showed that the structure and timing of milk feeds and solids were correct. However, she had decided to introduce certain foods that are more difficult to digest earlier than I recommend. Banana was added to his breakfast cereal when he was just five months. I advise introducing banana at six months and only once a baby has already tasted a good range of fruit and vegetables. Matthew loved banana and this prompted his mother to offer it to him regularly at lunchtime along with mashed avocado, another food that is hard to digest.

Matthew's mother had allowed him to take the lead with weaning, which meant he cut back too quickly on his daily milk intake. As a result, he was having to wake in the night to make up for the milk he was no longer getting during the day. It was clear from the feeding charts that Matthew had cut back too dramatically on his milk intake during the day, because his solids had been increased too rapidly (especially at breakfast). This in turn affected the amount of milk he was taking at lunchtime.

I advised Matthew's mother to cut back the breakfast cereal to two teaspoonfuls, with one or two cubes of pear or peach purée, instead of five teaspoonfuls of breakfast cereal and mashed banana. Lunch, which also consisted of hard-to-digest fruits such as avocado and banana, was replaced with 4–6 cubes of vegetable purée, as recommended in my feeding plans. After the 6pm milk feed I suggested that Matthew be given 4–6 tablespoons of baby rice mixed with two cubes of fruit purée, instead of vegetable purée.

Within three days Matthew was back to sleeping from 7pm–7am. This problem of milk underfeeding was caused by introducing too much of the wrong types of food too early or at the wrong time. This is a very common mistake and is the main reason for babies cutting back too quickly on their daytime milk, which results in a genuine need to feed in the night.

Bronwen: aged six months

Bronwen was exclusively breast-fed from birth, apart from one formula feed at 10pm, and she happily followed the CLB routines in my first book from the age of two weeks. Although Bronwen's mother had never expressed at the times I suggested, Bronwen was sleeping through the night to 7am from her 10pm feed at the age of eight weeks. Her mother was advised to wean her at four months and, because her mother was planning to return to work part-time when Bronwen was six months, she also introduced a bottle of formula at the 2.30pm feed. Bronwen was very reluctant to take the bottle and would never drink more than 90ml (3oz). However, her weight gain was still good and she continued to sleep from 7pm–7am.

At six months, when Bronwen's mother returned to work, she introduced protein at her 11.30am feed and dropped the milk. Bronwen was now having a breast-feed at 7am and 6.30pm, and a bottle of formula at 2.30pm. Within a week of the new feeding pattern commencing, Bronwen began waking up at 5am. Her mother attempted to settle her back to sleep by patting her or offering her water, but this rarely worked. Such an early start to the day resulted in Bronwen being very grumpy and overtired by the time her mother returned home from work at 5pm.

When I received Bronwen's feeding chart, it was obvious that the reason for her 5am waking was one of genuine hunger caused by the sudden drop in her daily milk intake. I believed that there were two reasons for the reduction in her milk intake. The first was that, unlike most babies, Bronwen did not automatically increase the amount she drank at her 2.30pm feed when the 11.30am feed was dropped. The second reason was that her mother's milk supply had decreased very rapidly when she started work and went down to two feeds a day. This meant that in addition to the too-small feed at 2.30pm, Bronwen was not getting enough milk at the 6.30pm feed, resulting in a genuine need to feed at 5am.

Unfortunately, because Bronwen had been given a bottle so infrequently and refused to drink a top-up after the 6.30pm feed, and because she was only taking the smallest amount from a bottle at 2.30pm, her mother had to continue to feed her at 5am.

When she eventually decided to wean her completely on to formula feeds, I suggested that she should first replace the morning feed with a bottle, before the evening one. Because Bronwen had gone for a longer spell without food she would be less likely to fight the bottle. Once she was totally weaned on to formula, she started to sleep through until 7am again.

I believe that this problem could have been avoided if Bronwen's mother had continued to express at 9.30–10pm, which would have helped keep up her milk supply. Also, because she knew she was returning to work, it would have been better to get Bronwen used to taking a full feed from a bottle at a much earlier stage.

Your questions answered

Q Why do you advise introducing solids at the 11am feed? Many of my friends who have weaned their babies started doing so after the first feed in the morning or after the 2/2.30pm feed.

A • I always start solids at the 11am feed as it is easier to push the 11am feed to a proper lunch at 12 noon than to try to bring the solids forwards from 2/2.30pm to noon. Also, if you have been advised to wean your baby before the age of six months, milk is still the most important source of food for your baby, providing him with the right balance of vitamins and minerals. By giving your baby his first solids after the 11am feed you can be reassured that he has had nearly half of his daily intake before noon.

• If you start solids at 2/2.30pm it could put him off the 6pm feed and make him cut back too much on it. If he does cut back on the 6pm feed, he may wake earlier for his 10pm feed, which could have a knock-on effect on the time he wakes in the morning.

• Solids are introduced once milk is no longer satisfying your baby's hunger. If you introduce them first after the 7am feed instead of the 11am, it could mean he would take a smaller milk feed at this time. Because milk alone is no longer satifying his appetite it could mean that his lunchtime nap becomes affected and he may wake up earlier due to hunger. If his 11am feed is reduced it could also result in him taking too big a feed at 2/2.30pm, and cutting back at the 6pm feed, which could affect his night-time sleep.

• Starting solids at the 11am feed will also make it easier to establish three solid meals a day. The majority of babies wake between 6am and 7am, and when breakfast is introduced it usually comes between 7am and 8am. As their need for solids increases it becomes very difficult to get them to wait until 2/2.30pm for their next lot of solids. This can result in two problems: the baby's need for the 11am milk feed increases; instead of decreasing, which can result in his taking less milk or solids at 2/2.30pm, and getting hungry long before his next feed;

alternatively, if you decide to bring the 2/2.30pm feed
forward it means the baby's lunchtime nap will be cut
short. Either way you could end up with a baby who is
very grumpy all afternoon because he is too tired or too
hungry.

Q   **I was advised to wean my baby of five and a half months
early as he weighs over 7.7kg (17lb). He is following the
feeding plan well at 11am, but he gets very tired by
6.15pm and he will take his full milk feed but is too
irritable to take the baby rice, and he has now started
waking up at 9pm looking for a big milk feed. He has also
started to cut back on his morning feed since his late feed
has increased.**

   **I have tried moving the rice to 5pm, but he then cuts
back on his 6.15pm feed, and again needs to feed at 9pm,
with the same result – he cuts back on his morning feed.**

A   • I would try giving him two-thirds of his milk feed at
      5.30–5.45pm followed by his baby rice, and wait until
      6.30pm before starting his bath. Although he will be
      getting tired, the bath should revive him just enough to
      take the remainder of his milk feed at around 6.50pm.

   • As he gets a little older he should begin to get less tired at
      6.15pm. When this happens, try giving him half of his
      baby rice at 5pm, a bath at 6pm, then his full milk feed,
      followed by the remainder of the baby rice.

   • By the time he gets to six months you should be able to
      transfer all of his solids to 5pm, and give him a full milk
      feed after his bath. However, should you find he begins
      to wake earlier in the morning it may be advisable to go
      back to splitting the solid feed for a further two or three
      weeks.

Q   Which is the best food to introduce first?

A   • The reason we wean babies is because milk alone no longer
satisfies their hunger, and in my experience, baby rice does
this best. Baby rice is also very bland and makes the
transition from milk to solids easier. If baby rice is tolerated
I would then introduce some pear purée (page 53) and if
the baby had no adverse reaction, I would always mix a
small amount of pear with the baby rice. This will help prevent him from becoming constipated, which can happen to
some babies when solids are first introduced.

• Once these two foods are established, it is best to
concentrate on introducing a variety of vegetables as
described on page 17. Research has shown that babies
weaned on fruit are less likely to thrive than those weaned
on baby rice. Most experts advise that all babies should
start weaning on baby rice.

• If you have been advised to wean before six months it is
important that you introduce new foods every 3–4 days.
If you start weaning at six months you can progress
through the first stage foods much more quickly,
introducing new foods every couple of days.

• I also believe that it is very important to wean babies on
home-made food as opposed to jars of fruit and vegetables.
The taste of commercial baby food, no matter how pure, is
always different from that of food cooked at home. I have
also found that babies who are weaned on fresh home-
made food are much less likely to become fussy eaters.

Q   How will I know how much solid food to give my baby?

A   • If you are weaning before six months, milk is still the
most important part of your baby's diet, and once solids
are introduced he will need a minimum of 600ml (20oz) a

day. During the first month if you always offer the milk first, then the solids, you can be sure he will take exactly the amount of solids he needs. This will prevent him from replacing his milk too quickly with solids.

• Between four and five months most babies should ideally be having four full milk feeds between 7am and 7pm, and some may still need a small milk feed at 10pm. (A full feed is defined as a formula-feed of 240ml/8oz or a breast-feed.) As your baby increases his solids during the day he should start to reduce the amounts he takes at 10pm, and most babies will cut this feed out by five months of age if they have been weaned early.

• If you are weaning at six months your baby will probably still be on 4–5 milk feeds a day. Because you will be establishing solids much more quickly you would need to cut back very rapidly on the milk feed at 11am to ensure that your baby is interested in solids. Once solids are introduced at 11am and in the evening, he should start to cut down and eventually cut out his late feed. If he does not cut down on this feed he could become very resistant to the introduction of solids. If your baby does not show signs of cutting back on the late feed of his own accord you can use the method described on page 29, provided he is sleeping until nearer 7am.

• Although all babies' appetites are different, and how quickly your baby increases his solids will depend on the age he was when you first introduced solids. Babies weaned early will increase their solids at a slower pace than babies who started weaning at six months. However, between six and seven months most babies will have reached a stage where they are taking between 6–8 cubes of vegetables and protein at lunchtime, and 6–8 teaspoonfuls of baby rice plus two cubes of vegetable or fruit purée in the evening.

- Most will also be taking a small amount of cereal and fruit at breakfast time. Very small babies may be taking less than this and very large babies may need slightly more. Be guided by your baby.

- If you are weaning your baby before six months the most important thing to remember during this first month of weaning is that any solid food you give your baby should be in addition to the milk, not as a replacement for it. A baby who is taking a lot more than the quantities I have recommended, and cuts right back on his milk, will be losing valuable nutrients that he gets from his milk. Remember, solids at this stage are really first tastes and fillers, not meals.

Q **When should I start to reduce the amount of milk my baby drinks?**

A   • Until your baby is weaned he will need between four and five full feeds a day, which could mean anything between 600ml (20oz) and 900ml (30oz) a day. Once solids are introduced he will still need a minimum of 600ml (20oz) a day.

- When solids are introduced at six months you should go straight into the tier method of feeding, giving him half the milk feed first, then some solids, followed by more milk. This will encourage your baby to cut back slightly on his milk feed and increase his solids, preparing him for a feeding pattern of three meals a day between six and seven months.

- Once solids are established in the evening your baby should automatically cut back on the 10pm feed if he is still having one. If he is not I would suggest that you increase his solids, and gradually decrease this feed using the method described on page 29.

- With breast-fed babies a feed from one breast can be classed as half a milk feed.

Q   **Which foods are most likely to cause allergies and what are the symptoms?**

A   • The most common allergy-causing foods are cow's milk products, wheat, fish, eggs, citrus fruits and nuts. Some experts believe that in families with a history of allergies, introducing these foods should be delayed until nearer eight months – particularly wheat and dairy products, which are the two foods that seem to be the main cause of most allergies. If there is a history of allergies in your family it would be wise to discuss this with your health visitor before introducing the above foods.

• Symptoms of allergies include rashes, wheezing, coughing, running nose, sore bottom, diarrhoea, irritability and swelling of the eyes.

• Keeping a detailed diary when you are weaning can be a big help when you are trying to establish the cause of any of the above symptoms.

• Any of the symptoms above can also be caused by house mites, animal fur, wool and certain soap and household cleaning agents. If in doubt, always check with your doctor to rule out any other possible causes or illness.

Recipes for first stage weaning

Ultra-smooth fruit and vegetable purées make ideal first stage weaning foods, and have the added advantage that they can be made in advance in batches, then frozen and defrosted when necessary. Freeze the purées in sections of an ice cube tray, then, as weaning progresses, you can increase the amount from one to two, three or more cubes per meal. Once weaning is well under way, different-flavoured cubes can be combined.

All the recipes described in the following pages can be frozen.

If you choose, you can substitute steaming for boiling, but always ensure vegetables are tender. See pages 13–14 for general advice on freezing and defrosting.

GENERAL TIPS

• About eight weeks after weaning has begun you can begin to introduce your baby to uncooked fruit purée.

• If your blender or food processor purées the skin finely, you can stop sieving foods from seven months and as weaning gets well under way, begin to make purées slightly coarser by mashing ripe fruit with a fork.

• The riper the fruit, the more naturally sweet it is.

Pear purée

Makes about 20 cubes

• 1kg (2lb 4oz) **dessert pears**

1. Wash the pears under cold running water, cut into quarters, remove core and any pith. Peel and put in a saucepan and cover with freshly boiled, filtered water. Bring to the boil, cover, then lower the heat and simmer for 5–7 minutes or until tender. Remove from the cooking liquid and purée to a smooth texture in a blender or food processor, using some of the cooking liquid to get the right consistency. Allow the mixture to cool.

2. Spoon the mixture into ice cube trays and put in the freezer. Leave to open-freeze for 3–4 hours or until fully frozen. Remove the cubes and put into clearly labelled freezer bags. Return to the freezer and use when necessary, defrosting thoroughly before use.

Carrot purée

Makes about 25 cubes

- 1kg (2lb 4oz) **carrots**

1. Wash the carrots under cold running water. Top and tail and either scrub well or peel. Put them in a saucepan and cover with freshly boiled filtered water. Bring to the boil, cover, then lower the heat and simmer for 12–14 minutes or until tender. Remove from the cooking liquid and purée in a blender or food processor, using some of the cooking liquid to get the right consistency. Allow the mixture to cool.

2. Spoon the mixture into ice cube trays and freeze as for pear purée (page 53).

Apple purée

Makes about 25 cubes

- 1kg (2lb 4oz) **eating apples**

1. Wash the apples under cold running water; quarter, peel and core them. Put all the prepared apples into a saucepan and cover with freshly boiled, filtered water. Bring to the boil, cover, then lower the heat and simmer for 5–7 minutes or until tender. Remove from the cooking liquid and purée to a smooth texture in a blender or food processor, using some of the cooking liquid to get the right consistency. Allow the mixture to cool.

2. Spoon the mixture into ice cube trays and freeze as for pear purée (page 53).

Sweet potato purée

Makes about 22 cubes

- 750g (1lb 8oz) **sweet potatoes**

1. Wash the sweet potatoes under cold running water, then peel. Put them in a saucepan and cover with freshly boiled, filtered water. Bring to the boil, cover, then lower the heat and simmer for 15 minutes or until tender. Remove from the cooking liquid. Mash the flesh with a fork, and press through a sieve. Allow the mixture to cool.
2. Spoon the mixture into ice cube trays and freeze as for pear purée (page 53).

Note: Ordinary potatoes can be substituted for sweet potatoes if preferred.

Courgette purée

Makes about 12 cubes

- 450g (1lb) **courgettes**

1. Wash the courgettes under cold running water. Cut off the ends and slice the courgettes. Put them in a saucepan and cover with freshly boiled, filtered water. Bring to the boil, uncovered, then lower the heat. Simmer uncovered for about 5–7 minutes or until tender. Remove from cooking liquid and purée in a blender or food processor to a smooth texture, using some of the cooking liquid to get the right consistency. Allow the mixture to cool.
2. Spoon the mixture into ice cube trays and freeze as for pear purée (page 53).

Swede purée

Makes about 16 cubes

- 1 small **swede**, weighing about 350 g (12 oz)

1. Wash the swede under cold running water. Peel and slice then dice into even-sized cubes. Put in a saucepan and cover with plenty of freshly boiled, filtered water. Bring to the boil, cover, then lower the heat and simmer for 10–12 minutes or until tender. Remove the swede from the pan and purée to a smooth texture in a blender or food processor, adding some of the cooking liquid to get the right consistency. Allow the mixture to cool.
2. Spoon the mixture into ice cube trays and freeze as for pear purée (page 53).

Green bean purée

Makes about 12 cubes

- 225 g (8 oz) **green beans**

1. Top and tail the green beans and remove the strings. Wash the beans in a colander under cold running water. Put them in a saucepan and cover with freshly boiled, filtered water. Bring to the boil, then lower the heat and simmer, uncovered, for 4–5 minutes or until tender. Remove from the pan and purée to a smooth texture in a blender or food processor, using some of the cooking liquid to get the right consistency. Allow the mixture to cool.
2. Spoon the mixture into ice cube trays and freeze as for pear purée (page 53).

Peach purée
Makes about 20 cubes

- 3 fresh ripe **peaches**
- 4 tbsp boiled filtered **water**

1. Wash the peaches under cold running water. Peel, halve and stone them and roughly chop the flesh. Put the flesh into a saucepan with the water. Bring to the boil, then cover, lower the heat and simmer for 10 minutes or until tender.

2. Remove from the cooking liquid and purée to a smooth texture in a blender or food processor.

3. Spoon the mixture into ice cube trays and freeze as for pear purée (page 53).

Note: Scale the amounts down to just 1 ripe peach and 1 tbsp boiling water if not planning to freeze the recipe.

Cauliflower purée
Makes about 30 cubes

- 1kg (2lb 4oz) **cauliflower**, cut into small florets

1. Wash the cauliflower florets under cold running water. Put into a saucepan and cover with freshly boiled, filtered water. Bring to the boil, then lower the heat and simmer, uncovered, for 8–10 minutes or until tender. Purée to a smooth texture in a blender or food processor, adding some of the cooking liquid to get the right consistency.

2. Spoon the mixture into ice cube trays and freeze as for pear purée (page 53).

Broccoli purée

Makes about 20 cubes

- 450g (1lb) **broccoli**, cut into small florets

1. Wash the broccoli florets under cold running water. Put into a saucepan of freshly boiled, filtered water. Bring to the boil, cover, then lower the heat and simmer for 4–6 minutes or until tender (test stalks). Remove from the cooking liquid and purée to a smooth texture in a blender, or food processor, adding some of the cooking liquid to get the right consistency. Allow the mixture to cool.

2. Spoon the mixture into ice cube trays and freeze as for pear purée (page 53).

Basic stocks

Home-made chicken stock

Makes 1 litre (1¾ pints)

- 1 **chicken carcass**
- 1 **onion**, peeled and quartered
- 1 **carrot**, peeled and diced
- 1 stick **celery** or half a **leek** (green top) (optional) sliced
- 1 **bay leaf** (optional)
- 2 litres (3½ pints) cold filtered **water**

1. Put all the ingredients into a large saucepan, bring to the boil then lower the heat, half-cover with a lid and simmer for 2 hours or until the liquid has reduced by half.

2. Strain the stock into a jug, cover and leave to cool. Store in the fridge and use within 24 hours, or freeze in small containers.

Home-made vegetable stock
Makes 1 litre (1¾ pints)

- 1 **onion**, peeled and quartered
- 2 **carrots**, peeled and diced
- 3 sticks **celery**, trimmed and sliced
- ½ **leek** (green top), sliced
- 1.5 litres (2½ pints) cold filtered **water**

1. Put all the ingredients into a saucepan, bring to the boil, then lower the heat, half-cover with a lid and simmer for 1 hour.
2. Strain the stock into a jug, discarding the vegetables. Cover and leave to cool. Store in the fridge and use within 24 hours, or freeze in small containers.

3 Second stage weaning: seven to nine months

During the second stage of weaning, the amount of milk your baby drinks will gradually reduce as his intake of solids increases. It is, however, important that he still receives a minimum of 540–600ml (18–20oz) a day of breast or formula milk. This is usually divided between three milk feeds and milk used in food and cooking as milk-based sauces are introduced. At this stage of weaning you should be aiming towards establishing three good, solid meals a day, so that by the time your baby reaches nine months of age, he is getting most of his nourishment from solids. During this time it is important to keep introducing a wide variety of foods from the different food groups (carbohydrate, protein, dairy, fruit and vegetables) so that your baby's nutritional needs are met (see page 17).

Most babies are ready to accept stronger-tasting foods at this age. They also take pleasure from different textures, colours and presentation. Food should be mashed or 'pulsed' and kept separate to avoid mixing everything up. Fruit need not be cooked; it can be grated or mashed. It is also around this age that your baby will begin to put food in his mouth. Raw soft fruit, lightly cooked vegetables and toast can all be used as finger foods. They will be sucked and squeezed more than eaten at this stage, but allowing your baby the opportunity to feed himself encourages good feeding habits later on. Once your baby is having finger foods, always wash his hands before a meal and never leave him alone while he is eating.

Between eight and nine months, your baby may show signs of wanting to use his spoon. To encourage this, use two spoons when you feed him. Load one for your baby to try and get the food into his mouth. You use the other spoon for actually getting the food in! You can help his co-ordination by holding his wrist gently and guiding the spoon into his mouth.

Foods to introduce

Dairy products, pasta and wheat can be introduced at this stage. Full-fat cow's milk can also be used in cooking, but should not be given as a drink until one year. Small amounts of unsalted butter can also be used in cooking. Egg yolks can be introduced, but must be hard-boiled. Cheese should be full fat, pasteurised and grated, and preferably organic. Olive oil can be used when cooking casseroles.

Tinned fish such as tuna may also be included, but choose fish in vegetable oil or spring water, as fish canned in brine has a higher salt content. A greater variety of vegetables can also be introduced such as coloured peppers, Brussels sprouts, pumpkin, cabbage and spinach. Tomatoes and well-diluted unsweetened fruit juices can be included if there is not history of allergies. All these foods should be introduced gradually and careful notes made of any adverse reactions.

Once your baby is used to taking puréed foods from a spoon, vegetables can be mashed rather than puréed. When he is happy taking mashed food, you can start to introduce small amounts of finger food. Vegetables should be cooked until soft then offered in cube-sized pieces or steamed and then mixed to the right consistency. As soon as your baby is managing softly cooked pieces of vegetables and soft pieces of raw fruit, you can try him with toast or a low-sugar rusk. By nine months, if your baby has several teeth he should be able to manage some chopped raw vegetables. Dried fruit can also be given now but it should be washed first and soaked overnight.

Breakfast

Sugar-free, unrefined wheat cereals can now be introduced; choose organic ones fortified with iron and B vitamins. You may want to delay introducing these if you have a family history of allergies – check with a health visitor or GP or a dietitian. Try adding a little mashed or grated fruit if your baby refuses them. Try to alternate the cereals between oat-based and wheat-based, even if your baby shows a preference for one over the other. You can encourage your baby with finger foods by offering him a little buttered toast at this stage. Once your baby is finger feeding, you can offer a selection of fruits along with lightly buttered toast.

Most babies are still desperate for their milk first thing in the morning, so still allow him two-thirds of his milk first. Once he is nearer nine months of age he will most likely show signs of not being hungry for milk and this is the time to try offering breakfast milk from a beaker.

Lunch

If your baby is eating a proper breakfast you will be able to push lunch to somewhere between 11.45am and 12 noon. However, should he be eating only a small amount at breakfast he will need to eat slightly earlier. Likewise, a baby who is having only a very short nap in the morning may also need to have lunch slightly earlier. It is important to remember that an overtired, over-hungry baby will not feed as well, so take a cue from him as to the timing of lunch.

During this stage of weaning you will have established protein at lunchtime. I usually find that during the early stages of introducing protein, cooking it as a casserole with root vegetables makes it much more palatable as many babies baulk at the strong flavour of protein which has been cooked on its own then mixed with vegetables.

Whenever possible, try to buy organic chicken and meat, which is free from additives and growth stimulators. Pork, bacon and processed hams should not be given as they have a high salt content. You should still continue to cook all food without additional salt or added sugar, although a small amount of fresh herbs can be introduced at around nine months of age.

Once protein is well established, your baby's milk feed should be replaced at lunchtime with a drink of cool boiled water or well-diluted juice from a beaker. You might find that he drinks only a small amount from the beaker and may look for an increase of milk in the 2.30pm milk feed, or an increase of cool boiled water later in the day.

If you are introducing your baby to a vegetarian diet, it is important to seek expert advice on getting the balance of amino acids right. Vegetables are incomplete sources of amino acids when cooked separately, and need to be combined correctly to provide your baby with a complete source of protein.

If your baby is still hungry after his main meal, offer a piece of cheese, a breadstick, chopped fruit or yoghurt.

Tea

Once your baby is finger feeding, tea can include a selection of mini sandwiches, rice cakes with spread or breadsticks. Some babies get very tired and fussy by teatime. If your baby does not eat much, try offering some rice pudding and fruit or a sugar-free yoghurt with fruit. A small drink of cool boiled water or well-diluted juice from a beaker can be offered after tea. Do not allow too large a drink at this time as it will put him off his last milk feed. His bedtime milk feed is still important at this stage. If he starts cutting back too much on this feed, check you are not overfeeding him on solids or giving him too much to drink.

Daily requirements

During the second stage of weaning it is important to work towards establishing three proper solid meals a day. Iron is a significant nutritional consideration at this time. This important mineral is essential for your baby's mental and physical development and for the formation of red blood cells. All babies are born with a natural store of iron in their bodies, but by the time they reach six months of age most of it will have been used up, so it is very important now to include iron-rich foods, such as red meat, green leafy vegetables, dried fruits and iron-enriched breakfast cereals, in his diet. To help improve absorption of foods rich in iron always try to serve them with vitamin C-containing fruits and vegetables, e.g. citrus fruits, berries or a small beaker of diluted pure fruit juice. Once you have established protein at lunchtime, it is important to drop the lunchtime milk feed – giving milk to drink with protein reduces iron absorption by up to 50 per cent.

Your baby still needs 540–600ml (18–20oz) of breast or formula milk a day, inclusive of milk used for mixing food. If he starts to reject his milk, cut right back on his 2.30pm milk feed to ensure that he takes a good milk feed first thing in the morning and at bedtime. Offer him extra yoghurt and cheese, and include milk-based sauces and puddings in his diet to ensure that his daily milk requirements are met.

Weaning guidelines

- Between the ages of seven and nine months your baby should have 2–3 servings of carbohydrates a day. These should be in the form of cereal, wholemeal bread, pasta or potatoes.

- Choose less-refined sugar-free cereals such as Weetabix or Ready Brek, which are rich in iron and vitamins. These can be served with fresh mashed or grated fruit.

- Your baby needs at least two servings of vegetables and fruit a day, with, ideally, more vegetables than fruit. Fruit need no longer be cooked or puréed. Start off by offering it grated and mashed, progressing to small pieces of soft bite-sized pieces.

- Your baby will need one serving of animal protein a day, a serving starting at approximately 25g (1oz) and increasing to around 50g (2oz). When serving a vegetarian meal, make sure you follow the guidelines for combining vegetable protein to ensure that your baby receives a complete protein meal. It is always wise to speak to your health visitor or a dietitian before giving a wholly vegetarian diet to your baby.

- Remove all fat, skin and bones from meat and poultry and avoid meats such as ham, pork and bacon which are too high in fat and salt. Continue to cook meats with vegetables in casseroles but these can now be pulsed together in the blender instead of being puréed into a totally smooth consistency.

- From six months onwards vegetables can be mashed instead of puréed. Once your baby is happy taking mashed, but not *lumpy*, food you can start to introduce small amounts of finger foods. Vegetables should be cooked until soft then offered in cube-sized pieces or steamed and then mixed to the right consistency with cool filtered water. Once your baby is managing softly cooked pieces of vegetables and soft pieces of raw fruit, you can try him with pieces of toast or a low-sugar rusk. By nine months, if your baby has several teeth, he should be able to manage some chopped raw vegetables. Dried fruit can be given now but it should be washed first and soaked overnight.

- Egg yolks can be introduced, but must be hard-boiled. Tinned fish such as tuna may also be included, but choose fish in vegetable oil or spring water, as fish canned in brine has a higher salt content.

- Once your baby is self-feeding it is important to wash his hands thoroughly before and after meals. He should never be left unattended once he is self-feeding because of the risk of choking.

- When protein is well established at lunchtime, the milk feed should be replaced with a drink of water or well-diluted juice

– try to encourage him to drink this from a beaker. Once he is happy to do this, introduce a beaker for his 2.30pm feed. By eight months, try to get him to take at least some of his breakfast milk from a beaker.

• At mealtimes, it is best to serve water or well-diluted pure juice after your baby has eaten most of his solids; that way the edge will not be taken off his appetite.

• Olive oil can be introduced in cooking between six and seven months and small quantities of herbs used in cooking from eight months.

• A very hungry baby who is taking three full milk feeds a day, plus three good solid meals, may need a small drink and a piece of fruit mid-morning.

• Small amounts of unsalted butter and full-fat cow's milk (preferably organic) can be used in cooking, but cow's milk should not be given as a drink yet as it is too low in iron.

• By the end of six months your baby will probably be ready to sit in a high chair for his meals. Always ensure that he is properly strapped in and never left unattended. Between eight and nine months he may show signs of wanting to use his spoon. To encourage this, use two spoons. Load one for him to try and get the food into his mouth and use the other to actually get the food in. You can help his co-ordination by holding his wrist and gently guiding his spoon into his mouth.

Menu planners at seven to nine months

If you have followed the plans for weaning at 6–7 months, your baby will now be eating protein at lunchtime. You now need to broaden his diet. It is very easy to get into the habit of serving the same favourite foods to your baby, but this could lead to him becoming very fussy about the foods he eats. I therefore advise that once your baby is established on the different protein meals, you should use the menu plans below as a guide to ensure that your baby receives a variety of foods and meals each week. The menus are to help you plan what your baby's meals might look like over a week. You can rotate them over a fortnight if you like, which will ensure your baby has a good range of different foods.

Menu A

Breakfast   Breast-feed or 210–240ml (7–8oz) of formula milk
plus
Wheat cereal with milk and mashed fruit *or*
Oat cereal with milk and mashed fruit *or*
Mixed mashed fruit and yoghurt, toast fingers, lightly buttered *or*
Wheat cereal with milk and finely chopped fruit *or*
Baby muesli with milk

Lunch   Bumper macaroni cheese (page 92) *plus*
Chopped fruit and yoghurt *or*
Individual fish pie (page 93) and sweetcorn *or*
Chicken casserole (page 85) and green beans *or*
Lamb hotpot (page 94) *or*
Chicken risotto (page 79) *or*
Fish Lyonnaise (page 87), carrots and peas *or*
Individual fish pie and broccoli florets
Drink of water or well-diluted juice from a beaker

Mid-afternoon   Breast-feed or 150–210ml (5–7oz) of formula milk

Tea   Thick courgette and leek soup (page 84) with rusks, lightly buttered *or*
Creamy pasta with spring vegetables (page 80) *or*
Baked potato with mashed baked beans *or*
Leek and potato soup (page 95) with bread, rusks or rice cakes, lightly buttered *or*
Corn chowder (page 91) *or*

Vegetable broth (page 86) and mini sandwiches *or*
Minestrone soup (page 82) with rice cakes, lightly
buttered
Drink of water from a beaker

Bedtime   Breast-feed or 180–240ml (6–8oz) of formula milk

Menu B

Breakfast   Breast-feed or 210–240ml (7–8oz) of formula milk
in a beaker *plus*
Wheat cereal with milk and finely chopped fruit *or*
Oat cereal with milk and grated fruit *or*
Mixed chopped fruit and yoghurt *or*
Baby muesli with milk *or*
Wheat cereal with milk and mashed fruit *or*
Oat cereal with milk and finely chopped fruit *or*
Mixed mashed fruit and yoghurt

Lunch   Chicken casserole with diced potatoes and broccoli
or
Vegetable shepherd's pie (page 97) *or*
Lamb hotpot *or*
Fish Lyonnaise with courgettes and carrots *or*
Tuna pasta (page 81) *or*
Quick chicken and vegetable gratin (page 83), green
beans and diced potatoes *or*
Bumper macaroni cheese *or*
Chicken risotto with chopped Brussels sprouts
Drink of water or well-diluted juice from a beaker

Mid-afternoon   Breast-feed or 150–210ml (5–7oz) of formula milk

Tea   Thick lentil and carrot soup (page 96) with mini
sandwiches *or*
Vegetable broth and mini sandwiches *or*
Creamy pasta with spring vegetables *or*

Thick courgette and leek soup, with rice cakes, lightly buttered *or*
Spotty couscous (page 90) *or*
Mixed root medley (page 88)
Drink of water from a beaker

Bedtime   Breast-feed or 180–240ml (6–8oz) of formula milk

Susannah: aged seven months

Susannah, who was bottle-fed from birth, would wake up screaming every hour and a half in the night, and was fretful and miserable for most of the day. When she was three months old, her exhausted parents decided to buy *The New Contented Little Baby Book*. They later admitted to being both suspicious and sceptical about my advice and techniques, which contradicted all the other books they had consulted. However, as the other advice hadn't worked, desperation led them to follow my routines to the letter. Within three days, Susannah was sleeping through the night and had become a happy and contented baby during the day. This pattern continued for two months.

Then, when Susannah outgrew her Moses basket at five months of age, her parents decided that they would move her 20-month-old sister Martha into a bed and give her cot to Susannah. She continued to sleep well when moved to the big cot, but the move from the cot to a bed for Martha turned out to be a disaster and resulted in weeks of hysterical crying and sleepless nights for her.

While the situation with Martha was becoming steadily worse, exhaustion led her mother to neglect Susannah's diet and routine. She was just given jars of baby food rather than the fresh food which had been an essential part of her dietary requirements. She also started to cut out her bath and massage in the evening. Soon, Susannah started waking every night at 10pm for a feed, which she had dropped a good six weeks back and, worse still, she would be woken by her sister's cries in the night. Her mother ended up giving her a formula-feed in the night so that she would settle quickly and allow her to return to an hysterical Martha.

This excessive night-time milk feeding resulted in Susannah eating even fewer solids than usual. She would take only a small amount of cereal after her morning bottle, the equivalent of two cubes of vegetables at lunchtime, and two teaspoonfuls of baby rice at teatime. This amount of solids was too small and did not include any form of protein, which is essential for a baby aged seven months and weighing nearly 7.7kg (17lb).

Although she was exhausted trying to deal with two sleepless children, Susannah's mother followed my advice and made two batches of red lentil savoury and two batches of chicken casserole. Within two days of introducing this food at lunchtime, Susannah began to drink less in the night. She gradually increased her lunchtime solids to six cubes of red lentil savoury or chicken casserole, and her teatime baby rice and fruit from two teaspoonfuls to six teaspoonfuls. These amounts were much more realistic for a baby of Susannah's age and weight. Although she did continue to wake around 10pm for a further four nights, because her appetite was being satisfied during the day her mother managed to settle her back to sleep quickly without feeding her. Very soon, Susannah was back to sleeping soundly from 7pm to 7am.

I believe that the main cause of Susannah waking and wanting to feed in the night was due to her not receiving the correct amounts of the right sorts of food during the day. In my experience, the occasional use of convenience food is fine, but babies who are being fed consistently from jars and packets are much more likely to develop sleeping problems related to feeding.

Emily: aged eight months

Emily had successfully followed the Contented Little Baby routines since she was three weeks old, sleeping through the night from the 10pm feed at eight weeks. When solids were introduced at six months Emily quickly dropped the 10pm feed and slept well from 7pm to 7am. She continued to sleep and eat well until she reached seven months. She then caught a bad cold that lasted for over two weeks and resulted in lots of sleepless nights. She also started to get very fussy about her food, refusing lots of the home-cooked meals that her mother normally gave her. Desperation and concern over her poor appetite and exhaustion from weeks of sleepless nights resulted in Emily's mother giving her commercial baby food at some mealtimes. Once Emily's cold had disappeared her appetite began to improve and she very quickly developed a taste for the jars of baby food. Her mother was so pleased to see her eating normal quantities again that she started using more and more jars.

However, despite getting over her cold and eating well, Emily continued to wake up in the night, and became increasingly difficult to settle. Even when she had the cold Emily had never been fed in the night, although she had been offered cool boiled water. Her mother was convinced that the continued wakings could not be due to hunger, but began to get very worried when Emily started drinking more and more water in the night – on some occasions she could drink as much as 180ml (6oz). On hearing her story I was not convinced that Emily's nutritional needs were being met during the day, as I had seen an increasing incidence of night-time waking in babies of her age who were being fed on jars of commercial baby food.

I explained to Emily's mother that although her daughter was taking the same quantity of commercial food as the amount she was taking of home-made food prior to her cold, the density of the food she was now having was totally different. A huge number of commercial baby meals have a high water content, and include sugar, maltodextrin and other modified starches that are used to thicken and bulk up the ingredients. The jars of chicken and lamb casserole that Emily was eating contained much less protein than the recipes her mother had been cooking for her before she caught her cold.

I convinced Emily's mother to go back to giving her home-cooked meals. However, because Emily had now developed a taste for the commercial baby food, we had to re-introduce the home-made versions very slowly. Emily's mother cooked similar recipes to her favourite jar meals, and froze them in quantities of half to one ice cubes. She would then very slowly introduce the home-cooked food cubes into the commercial meals, gradually increasing the amount of home-cooked food when she saw that Emily was happy taking it. It took nearly one month to get Emily totally back on to home-cooked food, but during that time her sleeping got better and she had fewer wakings in the night. By the time she was fully on a diet of home-cooked food she was back to sleeping a full 12 hours.

I have dealt with hundreds of problems similar to Emily's. While I believe the occasional use of commercial baby food does not create problems, I am convinced that its over-use may be the cause of poor sleeping habits with some babies.

Patrick: aged nine months

Patrick weighed nearly 4.5kg (10lb) at birth and went straight into the 2–4 week routine. He breast-fed well during the day, and slept through the night at four weeks, after his formula-feed at 10pm. He continued to sleep and feed well, following the routines to the letter until he was nearly nine months. It was at this stage that his parents rang me for advice, as things were going seriously wrong with Patrick's feeding. Between eight and nine months of age, he went from being an enthusiastic eater to being a fretful and fussy eater, refusing even his favourite dishes.

I immediately went to spend the day with him to try and sort out the problem. When I arrived, Patrick was playing; he was crawling well and had developed good hand-eye co-ordination, using the pincer grip to pick up and examine many of his smaller toys. He particularly enjoyed his shape-sorter toys, attempting to fit the various shapes into the appropriate holes, and got very cross when his mother attempted to help him do this. Patrick's behaviour showed he was clearly very advanced both mentally and physically and had a very independent streak.

This independent streak became more obvious during lunch. From the minute Patrick was placed in his high chair, he started to get fussy and fretful and would shake his head from side to side when his mother attempted to feed him. With a struggle, his mother managed to get Patrick to take half of the food in the bowl which, to my surprise, was still of a mashed consistency. Patrick's mother had always followed my books to the letter, and so I was intrigued to find out why she had not followed my advice of introducing chopped food by the age of nine months. She explained that she had tried this at seven months, but Patrick's keenness to self-feed meant lunch ended up taking nearly 45 minutes instead of the usual 30 minutes. This meant Patrick would go down for his mid-day nap later, which resulted in him becoming overtired and not sleeping so well.

Once Patrick was settled for his nap, I explained to his mother that self-feeding plays an important part in helping a baby develop physical and mental skills, by encouraging hand-eye co-ordination and improving their fine finger control, often referred to as the pincer grip. Patrick was encouraged to learn all these things during his play-time, then suddenly restricted at meal times, which must have caused him much confusion and frustration. At this age, babies become very aware of colour and texture, and I am sure that Patrick had become very bored with all his food being mashed up into one bowl.

For his tea that day, I suggested that we prepare a selection of cubed vegetables with small pasta shapes and allow Patrick to feed himself. There was much grabbing and squeezing of the food, and the meal was certainly more messy and took longer than usual, but Patrick happily ate everything that was put in front of him. Because he had been allowed to satisfy his feelings of independence, he happily allowed his mother to spoon-feed him the yoghurt and fruit that followed.

Once a baby starts to participate in feeding himself, it is important to allow extra time for his meals. I advised Patrick's mother to bring his lunch forward by 15 minutes, allowing a longer time until his self-feeding skills had improved.

Your questions answered

Q   When will I know if my baby is ready to reduce the
number of feeds he is having?

A   • The next feed to cut out during the second stage of
weaning would be the 11.45am/12 noon feed. Once your
baby is having protein at this meal he will not need a milk
feed. Using the tier method of feeding (page 18) at this
stage will ensure that your baby cuts down on the amount
of milk he drinks and increases the solids. I usually find
that once a baby is taking between six and eight level
tablespoons of food at lunchtime he will be happy to take
a drink of cool boiled water or well-diluted juice from a
beaker.

Q   My baby is six months old and is still taking four full feeds
a day. I have tried cutting back on the 11.45am milk feed,
but he screams and screams unless he gets a full feed,
which results in his refusing solids.

A   • Milk is still important during the second stage of weaning
but it would be advisable to try and reduce the amount
he is taking at the 11am feed so that he is getting a proper
protein lunch by the time he is seven months old.

• It may be that your baby is getting too tired to wait until
11.45am, and therefore finds it easier to satisfy his hunger
quickly by drinking all his milk first. As he is taking more
than his daily milk requirement in his other three feeds,
try bringing lunchtime back to 11.30am and offering him
his solids first, followed by the milk.

• Alternatively, bring his milk feed time right back to 11am.
He will not be quite so hungry so he may well cut back

on the amount he drinks, particularly when the amount he eats at breakfast increases. Leave a time space of at least 40 minutes before offering him the solids.

- If he reaches seven months and is still refusing solids, it would be wise to discuss with your health visitor whether this milk feed could be slightly diluted to help improve his appetite for solids. If she agrees, I would suggest that you still give the milk feed slightly earlier than the solids as the very sight of the bottle can be enough to put off some babies of this age eating their solids.

Q   When should I introduce a beaker and at which feeds?

A
- Once your baby reaches 6–7 months of age and is established on a proper protein meal at lunchtime he no longer needs milk at that feed and this would be a good time to introduce a beaker.

- He should be offered cool boiled water or well-diluted juice halfway through the meal and after every few mouthfuls. Many babies take quite a while to get used to drinking from a beaker and will only drink a very small amount in the first few weeks of its introduction. It is important to persevere. Experiment with different types of beaker until you find one that seems to suit your baby.

- If your baby is taking only a very small amount of fluid from a beaker at 11.45am, he may need to be offered extra milk at the 2pm feed or extra cool boiled water later in the day.

- Once he is accustomed to drinking water or well-diluted juice from a beaker, milk can be introduced in a beaker at either the 7am feed or the 2pm feed. This should ideally happen somewhere between the eighth and ninth month, preparing your baby for taking all his drinks from a beaker by one year.

• Experts recommend that all bottle-feeding is stopped by the age of one year, as it can remove the appetite for other foods. In my experience babies who continue milk-feeding from a bottle past the age of one year will often refuse milk altogether when the bottle is eventually stopped.

Q   When can I introduce cow's milk?

A   • Some experts advise that cow's milk can be introduced in small amounts in the preparation of solid foods from four months, and as a drink from one year. I personally prefer to wait until six months before introducing it in cooking, and if there is a history of allergies, I would wait even longer. If you are unsure about introducing cow's milk into your baby's diet, it would be wise to discuss the matter with your health visitor.

• All cow's milk, whether used in cooking or introduced as a drink at one year, must be full-fat pasteurised milk. Skimmed or semi-skimmed milk is not suitable for children under two years of age. In my opinion it is also advisable to use organic cow's milk.

Q   When can I stop puréeing my baby's food?

A   • Between six and seven months of age I start to mash or pulse the solids in a food processor. The consistency is not quite so smooth but it is without lumps. Most babies will simply gag on food if they are suddenly expected to go from eating very smooth food to food with lumps in it.

• Once your baby has got used to eating food with slightly more texture I would gradually mash or pulse it less and less until he will take food with lumps in it. By nine months most babies will happily eat food with a range of different textures and consistencies.

- Chicken and meat should still be pulsed very finely until your baby is around 10 months old, or shows signs of being able to chew it easily.

- If your baby refuses food with lumps in it, do not force the issue as it will only create eating problems. Instead make sure that you offer him lots of soft pieces of fruit and vegetables as finger foods. This will ensure that he makes the transition from puréed food to proper food just the same.

Q   When can I introduce finger foods?

A   • From seven months of age most babies are capable of eating a small amount of finger foods. Get your baby used to sitting in his high chair while you prepare his meal and place a variety of foods on his tray. At first much of the food will end up on the floor, but if you persist and always offer him a small selection, he will eventually start to eat some of it.

- Start by offering small pieces of softly cooked vegetables or pieces of soft fruit. I find that offering a tablespoon of mixed cooked frozen vegetables is often a successful way of getting babies interested in finger foods. The different colours and textures of the carrots, cauliflower and peas seem to attract them.

- Once your baby is managing vegetables and fruit, try offering a piece of lightly buttered toast, a low-sugar rusk, rice cake or breadstick.

- Once finger foods are introduced, always wash his hands before and after a meal, and never leave him alone while he is eating.

Recipes for seven to nine months

Making your own baby food needn't be fiddly or time-consuming if you make up large quantities at a time and store mini-meals away in the freezer. Build up a selection of small lidded plastic containers for this purpose, and vary the texture of the meals to suit your baby.

All the following dishes can be frozen except where stated. Those unsuitable for freezing make a delicious meal for baby and you. For general freezing and defrosting tips, see pages 13–14.

Chicken risotto

Makes enough for baby and you

Note: Not suitable for freezing

- 1 tbsp **olive oil**
- 200g (7oz) **chicken breast**, skinned, boned, rinsed and cubed
- ½ small **onion**, finely chopped
- 200g (7oz) **risotto rice**
- 250g (9oz) **butternut squash**, peeled, deseeded and diced
- 2–3 stems fresh **sage**
- 1 litre (1¾ pints) home-made **chicken** or **vegetable stock** (pages 58, 59) or filtered **water**

1. Heat the oil in a saucepan. Cook the chicken and onion for 5 minutes or until lightly browned.
2. Add the rice and continue frying for 1–2 minutes or until the rice looks transparent, then add the butternut squash, leaves torn from the sage stems and mix together. Pour over half the stock, stirring frequently. Bring to the boil, then cover, lower the heat and simmer for about 20 minutes, stirring frequently

during cooking and topping up with the remaining stock as needed until all the liquid is absorbed and the rice is creamy and soft or until the desired consistency is reached.

3. Purée in a blender or food processor, blending in batches if necessary, until the desired texture has been reached.

Creamy pasta with spring vegetables

Makes enough for baby and you

Note: Not suitable for freezing

- 150g (5oz) **carrot**, peeled and diced
- 150g (5oz) **broccoli**, cut into small florets, with stems sliced
- 75g (3oz) **green beans**, cut into three
- 75g (3oz) soup or baby **pasta**
- 75g (3oz) mild **Cheddar cheese**, finely grated
- 170–200ml (6–7floz) organic **full-fat milk**

1. Put the carrots in a steamer, cover and cook for 5 minutes.

2. Add the green vegetables and cook for 6–7 minutes or until all the vegetables are just tender and still brightly coloured.

3. Meanwhile, cook pasta in a separate saucepan of boiling filtered water for 6–7 minutes until tender or according to the packet instructions. Drain well.

4. Purée the vegetables and cheese in a blender or food processor, blending in batches if necessary, and gradually adding milk to achieve the desired consistency. Pour the vegetable sauce on top of the pasta.

TIPS
- If preferred, larger pasta shapes can be used instead – just increase the cooking times as necessary.

• As your baby gets older you may like to add a little chopped basil or marjoram to the dish for extra flavour.

• When your baby is happy to move on to coarser textures, continue to purée the vegetable and cream cheese mixture, then mix this with chopped pasta, leaving tiny soup pasta shapes whole.

Tuna pasta

Makes enough for baby and you

Note: Not suitable for freezing

- 50–75g (2–3oz) **pasta shapes**
- 1 tbsp **olive oil**
- 1 small **onion**, finely chopped
- 1 **garlic clove**, crushed
- 2 **tomatoes**, skinned, deseeded and finely chopped
- 1 tbsp **tomato purée**
- 100ml (3½floz) **apple juice** or filtered **water**
- 200g (7oz) can **tuna** in oil, drained and flaked
- 2–3 tbsp **fromage frais**

1. Add the pasta to a pan of boiling filtered water and cook for 10–12 minutes, or according to the packet instructions.
2. Heat the oil in a pan, add the onion and garlic, and cook for 3–4 minutes, stirring all the time.
3. Add the chopped tomatoes, the tomato purée, apple juice or water and the flaked tuna. Cook for a further 4–5 minutes.
4. Stir in enough fromage frais to make a creamy sauce.
5. Drain the pasta and mix with the tuna and sauce.

Minestrone soup
Makes 8–10 servings

- 1 tbsp **olive oil**
- 1 small **onion**, finely chopped
- 1 **garlic clove**, crushed
- 2 sticks **celery**, diced
- 2 **carrots**, peeled and diced
- 1 medium **potato**, peeled and diced
- 200g (7oz) can chopped **tomatoes**
- 1 **courgette**, washed and diced
- 75g (3oz) **green beans**, chopped
- pinch of **dried basil**
- 600ml (1 pint) home-made **chicken** or **vegetable stock** (pages 58, 59)
- 200g (7oz) can **haricot beans**, drained and rinsed
- 2 tbsp frozen **peas**
- 25g (1oz) small **pasta shapes**

1. Heat the oil in a pan, add the onion and garlic, and cook for 3–4 minutes.
2. Add the celery, carrots and potato and cook for a further 5–7 minutes, stirring occasionally.
3. Add the tomatoes, courgette, green beans, basil and stock to the pan, bring to the boil and simmer for about 25 minutes, or until the vegetables are tender.
4. Add the haricot beans, peas and pasta shapes and cook for a further 10–12 minutes.

Quick chicken and vegetable gratin

Makes 4–6 servings

- 1 tbsp **vegetable oil**
- 1 small **carrot**, peeled and diced
- ¼ small **red onion**, diced
- 25g (1oz) **mushrooms**, diced
- 2 tsp **plain flour**
- 4 tbsp **full-fat organic milk**
- 150ml (¼ pint) home-made **chicken** or **vegetable stock** (pages 58, 59) or filtered **water**
- 125g (4oz) **cooked chicken**, diced or minced
- 2 tsp finely chopped **fresh herbs**
- 2 tbsp **wholemeal breadcrumbs**
- 3 tbsp mild **Cheddar cheese**, grated
- knob of unsalted **butter**

1. Preheat the oven to 200°C/400°F/gas mark 6.
2. Heat the oil in a large saucepan and fry the carrots, onions and mushrooms together for 5–7 minutes or until softened. Stir in the flour and cook for 1–2 minutes. Gradually stir in the milk and the stock. Bring to the boil then lower the heat and simmer for 5 minutes. Stir in the chicken and the herbs and heat through for 5 minutes.
3. Spoon the chicken and vegetables into a shallow ovenproof dish and sprinkle the breadcrumbs and cheese and dot a little butter evenly over the top. Bake for 15–20 minutes or until golden brown. Serve mashed or puréed.

Thick courgette and leek soup

Makes 8–10 servings

- 1 tbsp **olive oil**
- 300g (10oz) **courgettes**, sliced
- 150g (5oz) **leeks**, chopped
- 2 **potatoes**, peeled and thinly sliced
- 1 **onion**, peeled and thinly sliced
- 2 large **tomatoes**, deseeded and chopped
- 900ml (1½ pints) home-made **vegetable stock** (page 59) or filtered **water**
- 1 **bay leaf**

1. Heat the oil in a saucepan, add the courgettes, leeks, potatoes and onion and sweat for 3–5 minutes, then add chopped tomatoes, vegetable stock and a bay leaf.
2. Bring to the boil, cover, then lower the heat and simmer for 25 minutes. Remove the bay leaf. Pulse or purée to a smooth texture in a blender or food processor, blending in batches if necessary.

TIPS

- Thick tasty soups make easy-to-eat suppers – ideal if your baby is feeling tired.
- Tomatoes can cause an allergic reaction in some babies, so keep a watchful eye on your baby if offering them for the first time.
- For older babies, flavour the soup with a sprinkling of fresh, frozen or dried herbs or a tiny amount of garlic and serve with fingers of toast.

Chicken casserole

Makes 6–8 servings

- 1 tbsp **olive oil**
- 1 small **onion**, finely chopped
- 2 organic **chicken breast fillets**, skinned, boned and cubed
- 2 **carrots**, peeled and diced
- 2 **parsnips**, peeled and diced
- 2 medium **potatoes**, peeled and diced
- 300ml (½ pint) home-made **chicken** or **vegetable stock** (pages 58, 59)

1. Preheat the oven to 180°C/350°F/gas mark 4.
2. Heat the oil in a pan, add the onion and cook until tender. Add the chicken and cook until sealed on all sides.
3. Transfer the chicken and onion to a casserole dish, add the diced vegetables and pour in the stock. Cover with a lid and cook in the oven for about 45 minutes or until the chicken and vegetables are tender.

Vegetable broth

Makes 8–10 servings

- 2 tbsp **olive oil**
- 1 small **onion**, finely chopped
- 2 **carrots**, peeled and diced
- 1 medium **leek**, finely chopped
- 1 medium **potato**, peeled and diced
- ½ small **turnip**, peeled and diced
- 900ml (1½ pints) home-made **chicken** or **vegetable stock** (pages 58, 59)
- 1 medium **carrot**, finely grated

1. Heat the oil in a pan, add the chopped onion and cook for 3–4 minutes.
2. Add the carrots, chopped leek, potato and turnip, and cook for a further 5 minutes.
3. Pour in the stock, bring to the boil and simmer for 30 minutes.
4. Add the grated carrot and simmer for a further 10 minutes, until the vegetables are very tender.

Fish Lyonnaise

Makes 4-6 servings

- 300g (10oz) **potatoes**, peeled and sliced
- 300g (10oz) **cod**, skinned and cubed
- 1 **onion**, very thinly sliced
- 50g (2oz) unsalted **butter**
- 300ml (½ pint) home-made **vegetable stock** (page 59)
  or filtered **water**
- 125g (4oz) mild **Cheddar cheese**, grated

1. Preheat the oven to 190°C/375°F/gas mark 5.
2. Arrange a layer of sliced potato in the bottom of a casserole
   dish, then put in a layer of the fish cubes followed by a layer
   of the sliced onion, dotted with butter. Continue to alternate
   the layers, finishing with a layer of fish, dotted with butter.
3. Cover with the vegetable stock, top with grated cheese and
   bake for 20–25 minutes.
4. Served mashed or puréed.

TIPS

- Although cod has very few bones, check carefully when cutting
  it into cubes to make sure they have all been removed.
- For older babies, mash the finished dish rather than puréeing
  it and add additional herbs such as a pinch of fresh, dried or
  frozen tarragon or chives – perhaps even a little tomato purée,
  too.

Mixed root medley

Makes 4–6 servings

- 200g (7oz) **parsnips**, peeled and cubed
- 200g (7oz) **carrots**, peeled and cubed
- 200g (7oz) **swede**, peeled and cubed
- 300g (10oz) **potato**, peeled and cubed
- 350ml (12floz) organic **full-fat milk**
- 150ml (¼ pint) boiling filtered **water**

1. Put all the vegetables into a saucepan with 300ml (½ pint) milk and the water. Cover and bring to the boil, then lower the heat and simmer for 20–25 minutes, stirring occasionally until the vegetables are tender.
2. Purée in a blender or food processor, blending in batches if necessary, gradually mixing in the remaining milk to achieve the desired consistency.

TIPS

- Cookers vary, so the amount of milk you will need when purée-ing may change. If your hob is difficult to turn down to a simmer, you will need all of the milk suggested, as more of the cooking liquid will be driven off during cooking.

- If the root vegetables are very dirty, rinse them again with boiling filtered water when diced.

Red lentil savoury

Makes 4–6 servings

- 75g (3oz) **red lentils**, rinsed
- 150g (5oz) **parsnips**, peeled and cubed
- 225g (8oz) **carrots**, peeled and cubed
- 350g (12oz) **potato**, peeled and cubed
- 600ml (1 pint) home-made **vegetable stock** (page 59) or filtered **water**

1. Put the lentils and root vegetables into a saucepan with the stock or measured water. Bring to the boil, cover, then lower the heat and simmer gently for 40 minutes or until the lentils are soft.
2. Purée in a blender or food processor, blending in batches if necessary, until smooth.

TIPS

- Wash the red lentils before use – they can be surprisingly dusty.
- As your baby gets older and more adventurous, try adding a pinch of ground turmeric, coriander and cumin to the recipe for extra flavour.
- Use butternut squash instead of the parsnip or carrot, if liked.

Spotty couscous

Makes enough for baby and you

Note: Not suitable for freezing

- ½ **orange** or **red pepper**, deseeded and finely diced
- 50g (2oz) **courgette**, finely diced
- 50g (2oz) **green beans**, finely sliced
- 50g (2oz) canned or frozen **sweetcorn**
- 100g (3½oz) **couscous**
- 2 tbsp **sultanas** or **raisins**
- 2 tsp **olive oil**
- 250ml (8floz) boiling filtered **water**
- 4 tbsp freshly squeezed **orange juice**

1. Cook the vegetables in a steamer for 5 minutes or until tender.
2. Meanwhile, put the couscous into a bowl with the sultanas, oil and boiling water. Cover with a plate and leave to absorb water for 5 minutes. Add the orange juice and fluff up with a fork.
3. Dice or mash the vegetables to the baby's desired texture. Stir into the couscous and spoon into bowls.

TIPS

- This easy supper is ideal for slightly older children and parents too. If making for the whole family, add seasoning once the baby's portion has been dished up.

- If you have mint growing in the garden, chop a little, well washed, and stir into the dish before serving.

- Fresh orange juice not only adds flavour, but the vitamin C it contains helps iron and calcium to be absorbed by the body.

Corn chowder

Makes 6–8 servings

- 350g (12oz) **potato**, peeled and diced
- 100g (3½oz) **carrot**, peeled and diced
- 1 small **onion**, finely chopped
- 350ml (12floz) organic **full-fat milk**
- 1 **bay leaf**
- 75g (3oz) frozen **sweetcorn**

1. Put all the ingredients except the sweetcorn into a saucepan. Bring to the boil, cover, then lower the heat and simmer for 10–12 minutes or until the vegetables are tender.
2. Add the sweetcorn to the pan and cook for 5 more minutes.
3. Discard the bay leaf, then purée the milk and vegetable mixture in a blender or food processor, blending in batches if necessary, until the desired consistency has been reached.

TIPS

- As your baby grows, simply mash the ingredients together and serve as a chunky soup-style meal with toast fingers.
- Canned sweetcorn can be used but make sure it has been processed without salt or sugar.

Bumper macaroni cheese

Makes 4 servings

- 100g (3½oz) **soup pasta**
- 25g (1oz) unsalted **butter**
- 25g (1oz) **plain flour**
- 350–400ml (12–14floz) organic **full-fat milk**
- 75g (3oz) fresh **young leaf spinach**
- 75g (3oz) mild **Cheddar cheese,** grated
- a little grated **nutmeg**

1. Cook the pasta in a saucepan of boiling water for 6–7 minutes (or according to packet instructions) until soft.

2. Meanwhile, melt the butter in a second saucepan, stir in the flour then gradually mix in 350ml (12floz) milk and bring to the boil, stirring until thickened and smooth. If too thick, add a little more milk.

3. Drain the pasta into a sieve, rinse and dry the pan. Wash the spinach well, shake off most of the water, then add to the dried pan and cook for 1–2 minutes until just wilted.

4. Take the spinach out of the pan, finely chop and stir into the sauce along with the cheese and nutmeg. Depending on the size of the pasta, finely chop or mash it to suit your baby.

TIPS

- As the pasta swells with standing, adjust the consistency with extra milk when reheating.

- Spinach can be a little strong-tasting on its own, so mix with a cheesy sauce to make it more acceptable for young diners.

Individual fish pies

Makes 6 servings

- 15g (½oz) unsalted **butter**
- 1 small **onion**, finely chopped
- 1 medium **leek**, thinly sliced
- 300g (10oz) **white fish fillets**, skinned
- 1 tbsp **plain flour**
- 300 ml (½ pint) organic **full-fat milk**
- 75g (3oz) mild **Cheddar cheese**, grated
- 25g (1oz) fresh white or brown **breadcrumbs**

1. Preheat the oven to 200°C/400°F/gas mark 6.
2. Melt the butter in a pan and sweat the onions and leeks for 3–4 minutes.
3. Cut the fish into cubes and place in small, lightly greased ramekins.
4. Stir the flour into the vegetables and cook for 2–3 minutes. Gradually add the milk, stirring all the time. Cook for a further 1–2 minutes until the sauce begins to thicken. Stir in 50g (2oz) of the cheese, then spoon the mixture over the fish.
5. Mix the breadcrumbs and the remaining cheese together, then sprinkle on top of each filled ramekin. Bake for 20 minutes until lightly golden and the fish is cooked.

Lamb hotpot

Makes 4–6 servings

- 250g (9oz) lean **lamb fillet**
- 1 tbsp **olive oil**
- ½ small **red onion**, chopped
- 300ml (½ pint) home-made **vegetable stock** (page 59) or filtered **water**
- pinch of dried **mixed herbs** or 2 tsp finely chopped **fresh herbs**
- 125g (4oz) **carrots**, peeled and diced
- 125g (4oz) **swede**, peeled and diced
- 125g (4oz) **potato**, peeled and diced

1. Wash the lamb under running cold water, dry with kitchen towel and cut into small cubes.
2. Heat the oil in a casserole dish and fry the lamb with the onion until the meat is browned.
3. Stir in the stock and herbs, add the vegetables and bring to the boil. Cover the casserole dish and simmer for 30 minutes.
4. Serve mashed or puréed.

TIPS

- If you have the oven on, cooking for the rest of the family, then this dish can also be casseroled at 180°C/350°F/gas mark 4 for 1–1¼ hours.
- For older babies, chop the finished dish or for toddlers, add tiny bite-sized dumplings.

Leek and potato soup

Makes 8–10 servings

- 25g (1oz) unsalted **butter**
- 450g (1lb) **leeks**, chopped
- 450g (1lb) **potatoes**, peeled and sliced
- 1 small **onion**, thinly sliced
- 1.1 litres (2 pints) home-made **vegetable stock** (page 59) or filtered **water**

1. Heat the butter in a saucepan. Add the vegetables and sweat for 3–5 minutes, then add vegetable stock. Bring to the boil, then lower the heat and simmer, uncovered, for approximately 25 minutes. Purée to a smooth texture in a blender or food processor, blending in batches if necessary.
2. If needed, add full-fat cow's milk to achieve the right consistency.

TIPS

- If you are worried about the amount of milk your child is drinking, use half-stock and half-milk in this recipe, or stir in some fromage frais or full-fat cream cheese after puréeing.

- Tired children find soup very comforting, and it can be quickly reheated – ideal if you have been out for the afternoon and need tea in a hurry.

- Serve with strips of toast or puff pastry shapes sprinkled with grated cheese as finger foods.

Thick lentil and carrot soup

Makes 6–8 servings

- 1 tbsp **olive oil**
- 1 small **onion**, peeled and thinly sliced
- 2 **carrots**, peeled and thinly sliced
- 1 **garlic** clove, peeled and chopped (optional)
- 200g (7oz) **red lentils**
- 1.1 litre (2 pints) home-made **vegetable stock** (page 59) or filtered **water**

1. Heat the oil in a large saucepan, add the onion, carrots and garlic, if using. Sweat for 3–5 minutes then add lentils and vegetable stock.

2. Bring to the boil, then cover, lower the heat and simmer for 30–35 minutes.

3. Purée to a smooth texture in a blender or food processor, blending in batches if necessary.

TIPS

- Red lentils make a great store-cupboard standby as they don't require pre-soaking like the other larger pulses and provide a good source of protein.

- For adventurous children you may also like to add a little ground cumin and coriander when cooking the lentils.

Vegetable shepherd's pie

Makes 6–8 servings

- 125g (4oz) unsalted **butter**
- 125g (4oz) **leeks**, trimmed, washed and finely chopped
- 1 **red onion**, finely chopped
- 175g (6oz) split **red lentils**
- about 500ml (18floz) home-made **vegetable stock** (page 59) or boiling filtered **water**
- 2 **tomatoes**, skinned and chopped
- 1 tsp dried **mixed herbs**
- 4 tbsp fresh **lemon juice**
- 900g (1¾lb) floury **potatoes**, peeled and cut into chunks
- 75g (3oz) mild **Cheddar cheese**, finely grated

1. Melt 50g (2oz) butter in a saucepan, add the leeks and onion and cook for about 8–10 minutes until softened.

2. Add the lentils and stir for 1–2 minutes to cover the lentils in the fat.

3. Add the stock or water, bring to the boil, then reduce the heat, half cover with a lid and simmer for about 15 minutes or until the lentils are soft, stirring occasionally. (There should be a little free liquid, so stir over a high heat to drive off any excess.) Cool slightly.

4. Remove the saucepan from the heat and stir in the tomatoes, herbs and lemon juice. Leave to cool.

5. Meanwhile, cook the potates in boiling water for 20 minutes or until tender. Drain well, then mash until smooth. Beat in the remaining butter and the cheese.

6. Preheat the oven to 200°C/400°F/gas mark 6.

7. Spoon the vegetable and lentil mixture into a 1.1-litre (2-pint) shallow oven-proof dish and level the surface. Spoon over the mashed potato.

8. Bake for 20–25 minutes until the topping is crisp and golden.

9. To serve, leave to cool slightly, then mash with a fork.

Third stage weaning: nine to twelve months

4

By the third stage of weaning your baby should be adopting a more adult style of eating. Most food should now be served mashed, chopped or diced, as it is important that he learns to chew properly at this stage. Once he has mastered the art of chewing lightly cooked vegetables and bite-sized pieces of soft fruit, try introducing raw vegetables and salads into his diet. A small amount of finger foods should be introduced at every meal and he should be encouraged to feed himself from the spoon, even if it means that meals take longer and he gets messier while eating. Eating should always be a pleasure for your baby and it is important that you allow him to take control of his eating habits at this stage, which often means that he will eat better at some meals than others. By the time he reaches one year of age he should be eating and enjoying a wide variety of food from the different food groups – carbohydrates, fruit and vegetables, and protein. It is important to continue to limit foods that are high in sugar and salt.

Breakfast

By the time your baby reaches one year he should be taking all his drinks from a beaker, so try to get him used to drinking some of his breakfast milk from a beaker by the time he reaches nine months. Once he is taking all his milk from a beaker the amount he drinks will probably go down to around 120–150ml (4–5oz), with 60–90ml (2–3oz) on his breakfast cereal. Some babies go through a stage of refusing their breakfast cereal at this age. If this happens, try offering yoghurt and fruit instead, followed by toast and butter or a fruit spread. Scrambled egg can also be offered once or twice a week.

Lunch

I have always found it better to give my babies their daily serving of protein at lunchtime as opposed to teatime. Babies of this age can often get very tired and irritable by 5pm and be a bit more fussy about eating. If they have had a well-balanced meal of protein and vegetables at lunchtime, you can be relaxed about what they have at teatime. If, for some reason, your baby doesn't have his daily serving of protein at lunchtime, include some grated cheese for tea.

Vegetables should be lightly steamed and chopped. Try to ensure that you vary the selection from day to day so that your baby is aware of the different colours and textures. It is also important not to overload his plate at this stage – an overfull plate can put some babies off, and with others can lead to a game of throwing food on the floor. Serve up a small amount and if he finishes it, offer more. If he does start to play up at mealtimes, refusing to eat or throwing his food on the floor, remove the plate immediately. It is very important not to get into a habit of force feeding or cajoling your baby to eat. Babies of this age very quickly learn to fuss and refuse their main course if they know they will be offered a treat such as fromage frais or a biscuit. If your baby doesn't eat well at lunchtime, offer him a piece of fruit or cheese mid-afternoon to see him through to teatime. A very hungry baby may need a serving of fruit and yoghurt in addition to his savoury lunch.

A drink of well-diluted, pure unsweetened orange or apple juice will help the absorption of iron at this meal. However, it is very important to try to get your baby to have most of his solids before offering him a drink. Allowing him to drink too much before his meal may considerably reduce his appetite.

By the end of the first year your baby should be able to eat much the same as the rest of the family and it is important that some of his meals are integrated with yours as this is how he will learn his table manners. When preparing family meals cook without salt, sugar and unnecessary additives, reserve the baby's portion, then add the desired flavourings for the rest of the family.

Tea

During the weaning stage your baby should be offered a wide variety of finger foods and teatime is the ideal meal to do this. Savoury sandwiches, small pieces of pizza and chopped-up vegetarian sausages are good examples of finger foods that can be given – served, say, with a thick soup, vegetable lasagne or vegetable bake. Many babies will cut right back or refuse their 2.30pm feed altogether at this stage. If you find that your baby's milk intake has dropped below 540ml (18oz) introduce foods such as cheesy vegetable bakes, mini quiches, baked potatoes with grated cheese or vegetables and pasta in a milk sauce at teatime. Fromage frais and milk puddings can also be offered at teatime if you are concerned about your baby's milk intake.

By one year of age your baby's minimum daily milk requirement will drop to 350ml (12oz) and the bedtime bottle should be replaced with a drink from a beaker. To get him used to less milk at this last feed offer him a small amount from a beaker with his tea, followed by a drink of 150–180ml (5–6oz) from a beaker at bedtime.

Daily requirements

During the third stage of weaning it is important that you encourage your baby to take all his milk from a beaker. Large volumes of milk should be discouraged after one year as they can take away the baby's appetite for solid food. Experts recommend that no more than 600ml (20oz) a day inclusive of milk used in food should be allowed. The majority of babies will be having 2–3 milk drinks a day at one year of age and need a minimum of 350ml (12oz) of milk each day, inclusive of milk used in cooking and on cereal.

By the age of one year your baby should be enjoying three well-balanced meals a day and be able to join in most of the family meals. Some babies may also need a snack mid-morning or -afternoon – try to offer healthy foods, avoiding biscuits, cakes and crisps.

Weaning guidelines

- Between the ages of nine and 12 months your baby should have 3–4 servings of carbohydrates a day in the form of cereals, wholemeal bread, pasta or potatoes.

- Your baby also needs 3–4 portions of fruit and vegetables, ideally taking more vegetables than fruit. By the end of the first year he should be eating a wide variety of raw and salad vegetables. The majority of his fruit and vegetables should now be offered chopped, sliced or cubed, instead of being mashed or puréed.

- Your baby will also need one serving of approximately 50g (2oz) animal protein a day or two servings of vegetable protein a day. Continue to avoid meats such as ham and bacon which are high in salt. Depending on how many teeth your baby has, most meat, poultry and fish should be chopped up into small pieces instead of being minced or mashed.

- Babies are very aware of colour and texture at this stage, so try to make food look appealing and interesting. Avoid mashing and mixing his different foods together, and make up a two-week menu plan to help you avoid giving the same foods too close together.

- If your baby is not taking his daily milk requirements between two or three feeds, increase the amount of cheese and yoghurt you give him. Also offer more sauces and puddings using milk.

- At mealtimes it is best to serve water or well-diluted pure fruit juice *after* your baby has eaten most of his solids so that the edge will not be taken off his appetite.

Menu planners at
nine to twelve months

Each of the menu plans below is a guide to what your baby's meals might look like over the course of a week. They ensure he receives a wide variety of food from all the food groups. You can follow one menu planner for a week, then rotate them over a fortnight.

Menu A

Breakfast   Breast-feed or a drink of formula milk from a beaker
plus
Wheat cereal with milk and finely chopped fruit *or*
Oat cereal with milk and finely chopped fruit *or*
Fruit yoghurt and toast fingers, lightly buttered *or*
Scrambled egg on toast *or*
Muesli with milk

Lunch   Fishy ribbons (page 110) and mixed vegetables *or*
Mini moussaka (page 111) *or*
Lamb and vegetable casserole (page 113) *or*
Mini salmon skewers (page 115) *or*
Chicken-peach casserole (page 117) *or*
Chicken with sweet peppers (page 119) *or*
Chicken and butter bean burgers (page 120)
Drink of water or well-diluted juice from a beaker

Mid-   Breast-feed or a drink of formula milk, water or well
afternoon   -diluted juice from a beaker

Tea   Vegetable broth (page 86) and mini sandwiches *or*
Leek and potato soup (pages 95) plus mini
sandwiches *or*
Pizza potatoes (page 114) *or*
Mixed vegetable frittata (page 116) *or*
Chinese noodles (page 118) *or*
Corn chowder (page 91)
Drink of water from a beaker

Bedtime   Breast-feed or 180ml (6oz) of formula milk

Menu B

Breakfast   Breast-feed or a drink of formula milk from a beaker
plus
Wheat cereal with milk and finely chopped fruit *or*
Oat cereal with milk and finely chopped fruit *or*
Scrambled eggs on toast *or*
Yoghurt and finely chopped fruit and toast fingers,
lightly buttered *or*
Baby muesli with milk

Lunch   Fish fingers, mixed vegetables and diced potatoes *or*
Mini moussaka *or*
Chicken and mushroom stir-fry (page 121) *or*
Beef and lentil pot supper (page 122) *or*
Chicken and vegetable oat crumble (page 123) *or*
Kiddie's kedgeree (page 124) *or*
Baby Bolognese (page 125)
Drink of water or well-diluted juice from a beaker

Mid-
afternoon   Breast-feed or a drink of formula milk, water or well-
diluted juice from a beaker

Tea   Minestrone soup (page 82) with rice cakes, lightly
buttered *or*
Thick lentil and carrot soup (page 96) with mini
sandwiches *or*
Baked beans on mashed potatoes *or*
Pizza potatoes (page 114) and mixed salad *or*
Chinese noodles and mixed salad *or*
Pick-up sticks (page 126)
Drink of water from a beaker

Bedtime   Breast-feed or 180ml (6oz) of formula milk

Theo: aged 11 months

Theo had always been a good feeder, enjoying a wide range of freshly cooked foods. At around eight months his mother noticed he was starting to reject more and more of his favourite meals. By the time she contacted me Theo had reached 10 months and mealtimes had become a complete battleground, with him clamping his mouth shut the minute a spoon was put anywhere near his mouth. His mother would try lots of different tactics to try and get him back to his old eating habits. She would spend ages singing, clapping and playing all sorts of games at mealtimes to try and get Theo to smile so he would take just one extra mouthful. If this approach failed she would then try offering him endless choices of meals, with him often taking no more than a mouthful from each choice.

When I received Theo's food diary I could see that there were several very obvious things that were not helping his feeding problems. One was the timing of his drinks, which were too close to mealtimes and taking the edge off his appetite; another was the fact that Theo was still drinking his morning and evening milk from a bottle. He was consuming over 240ml (8oz) at both of these feeds, which was also taking the edge off his appetite.

I advised Theo's mother to offer him no more than 180ml (6oz) from a beaker first thing in the morning and no more than 210ml (7oz) from his bottle in the evening. These amounts, along with milk used in cereals, would still exceed 350ml (12oz), the minimum recommended at one year of age. Any other fluid should be offered midway between meals, not an hour before. At mealtimes I advised that Theo should not be given his juice until he had eaten at least half of his solids.

It was also obvious from the food diary that most of Theo's food was still being mashed and mixed up and that very little finger food was being offered. I explained that babies of Theo's age become interested in the colour, texture and shape of their food and I suspected he had become very bored with all his food still being mashed and mixed up into one bowl. It was very important that he should be offered a selection of finger foods at most meals and that he should be allowed to feed himself, regardless of how messy he got.

Although I advise offering a selection of finger foods the choice should not be endless. At this age the amount a baby eats at individual meals can become very erratic and it is best never to try to force the baby to feed. Allow a certain length of time but if it becomes obvious that he is not interested, clear the food away. He should not be coaxed or cajoled into eating – all babies will eat well if they are hungry enough and not overtired. It is best to judge a baby's food intake over several days at this age, not by what he eats at individual meals.

Theo's feeding did improve considerably although he still had days when he was fussy. As he had just started learning to walk, I suspected that tiredness might also be a cause of his fussiness and I advised his mother to start his meals slightly earlier on days when he had been extremely energetic.

Your questions answered

Q   My baby is nine months old and has happily had three milk feeds a day of approximately 180–210ml (6–7oz) of formula each since he was six months old. He is now getting very fussy and fretful at his bedtime bottle, sometimes taking as little as 90ml (3oz), which has resulted in him waking earlier than 7am looking for a feed. I have tried cutting back on his 2.30pm feed but he gets very irritable and looks for his tea nearer 4.30pm instead of 5pm.

A
- Many babies do cut back or refuse a third milk feed at this stage. Obviously it is better if it is the mid-afternoon feed and not the last feed of the day. Continue to give your baby a reduced feed in the middle of the day but try offering him it at 3pm instead of 2.30pm and bring his tea forward to 4.45pm. Once he has increased his bedtime feed for several days you can try pushing his teatime solids back to 5pm. Do this gradually by two or three minutes every three days.

- If the above doesn't work it is also worthwhile looking at the amount of solids you are giving your baby at teatime. If he is having in excess of eight tablespoons of solids, try cutting back slightly, as this is another cause of babies cutting back too hard on their bedtime milk feed.

- Another reason for cutting back on the bedtime milk feed is overtiredness. It is at this age that many babies are beginning to crawl and pull themselves up. This extra physical activity can make them become very overtired at bedtime. It may be that your baby needs an extra 15 minutes' sleep at lunchtime so that he doesn't become overtired at bedtime. If he refuses the extra sleep you may find that bringing his bedtime routine forward by 15 minutes will help.

- If none of the above works, I would try cutting out the mid-afternoon milk feed altogether and replacing it with a drink of well-diluted juice or water and a snack, so he can get through to teatime. If he then drinks 180ml (6oz) in the morning and 180ml (6oz) in the evening, he will have reached the minimum amount. Extra milk on his cereal and in cooking should then easily meet his requirements.

Q   My baby is nearly 14 months of age and has happily drunk
     his milk in the morning and mid-afternoon from a beaker
     for over two months now. But he screams when I try to
     give him milk from a beaker at bedtime. He is taking
     nearly 240ml (8oz) at bedtime from the bottle and around
     180ml (6oz) from the beaker first thing in the morning
     and mid-afternoon. He has also started to get very fussy
     about his solids at breakfast, and on occasion has refused
     them altogether.

A   • During the third stage of weaning many babies will
       automatically cut out their third milk feed. When a baby
       continues to have three milk feeds at this age but starts to
       refuse solids it would be wise to gradually reduce the third
       feed, which should always be the mid-afternoon feed.

     • Gradually reduce the amount you give your baby to drink
       at 2.30pm and offer him a drink of milk from a beaker
       with his teatime solids instead. This should enable you
       gradually to reduce the amount he drinks from a bottle at
       bedtime.

     • After a couple of weeks when he is used to taking a small
       drink of milk from a beaker at teatime and his bedtime
       bottle is reduced to 150–180ml (5–6oz), try offering him
       that amount from a beaker.

     • At this age it often helps if parents have a drink from a
       beaker too, or if a favourite teddy is offered a drink from
       a beaker.

Q   When can I give cow's milk as a drink?

A   • Cow's milk can be given to drink once your baby reaches
       one year of age. It should always be full-fat and
       pasteurised. If possible, try to give your baby organic cow's
       milk as it comes from cows fed exclusively on grass.

• If your baby refuses cow's milk, I would try mixing it with formula: simply replace 25ml (1oz) of milk with formula. Gradually increase the proportion of cow's milk while decreasing the infant formula, until your child is drinking cow's milk only. If your child continues to refuse cow's milk, try a follow-on milk that tastes similar and can be used up to two years of age.

Q When should I encourage my baby to feed himself from the spoon?

A • By the time they reach 12 months, the majority of babies will be capable of getting some of their food into their mouth using their spoon. Spoon-feeding will be made easier for your baby if the food is served in a bowl as opposed to a plate.

• Once your baby is capable of feeding himself with a spoon mealtimes will probably take longer so allow extra time. Always supervise your baby during mealtimes. Never, ever leave him alone.

• Mealtimes can become extra messy once your baby is self-feeding. It is very important to remain very patient at this stage – the most important thing is that he eats well, regardless of how he gets the food into his mouth.

Recipes for nine to twelve months and over

As your baby's taste develops, you can begin to cook for all the family. However, you need to remember not to add any salt to the meals until you have set aside your baby's portion. Note that recipes unsuitable for freezing make one serving each for baby and you.

Fishy ribbons

Makes 2 servings

- 125g (4oz) **cod or haddock fillet**, skinned and rinsed
- 1 **egg**
- 40g (1½oz) fresh white or brown **breadcrumbs**
- 1 tbsp freshly grated **Parmesan cheese** (optional)
- 1 tbsp **sunflower oil**

1. Cut the fish into finger-sized strips. Beat the egg on a plate. Mix the breadcrumbs and Parmesan, if using, on another plate. Dip the fish strips into the egg and roll in crumbs until well coated. Put on a plate, cover and chill for at least 30 minutes.

2. When ready to cook heat the oil in a frying pan, add the fish strips a few at a time and cook for 3–4 minutes, turning several times until the breadcrumbs are golden brown and the fish turns white and flakes easily.

3. Drain the fish on to kitchen paper.

TIPS
- Use this same idea to make chicken ribbons, using strips of boneless, skinless chicken breast fillet.
- If serving with ketchup, go for the low-sugar and low-salt varieties.

Mini moussaka

Makes 4 servings

- 250g (9oz) lean minced **lamb**
- 1 small **onion**, finely chopped
- 100g (3½oz) **aubergine**, diced
- 1 clove **garlic**, crushed
- 175g (6oz) **courgette**, diced
- 300g (10oz) **passata** or finely chopped **tomatoes**
- 300ml (½ pint) filtered **water**
- pinch of ground **cinnamon** and **allspice**

Topping:

- 350g (12oz) baking **potatoes**, peeled
- 1 tbsp unsalted **butter**
- 1 tbsp **plain flour**
- 150ml (¼ pint) organic **full-fat milk**
- 25g (1oz) mild **Cheddar cheese**, grated
- 1 tbsp freshly grated **Parmesan cheese**

1. Preheat the oven to 200°C/400°F/gas mark 6.
2. Dry-fry the mince, onion and aubergine together until browned. Stir in the garlic and courgette, then add the passata, water and spices. Cover and bring to the boil, stirring, then lower the heat and simmer for 35 minutes.
3. Meanwhile, thinly slice the potatoes and cook in boiling filtered water for 4–5 minutes or until just tender. Drain well.
4. Put the butter, flour and milk into a small saucepan and bring to the boil, whisking continuously until thickened and smooth. Stir in the Cheddar cheese and set aside.
5. Divide the mince mixture between 4 small ovenproof dishes.

Pour some cheese sauce over each one. Arrange potatoes over the top and sprinkle with Parmesan. Cool and freeze at this stage.

6. Bake for 25 minutes or until the top is golden brown. Serve with just-cooked green beans or broccoli florets.

TIPS

- The mince mixture can be casseroled in the oven at 180°C/350°F/gas mark 4 for 1¼ hours, if preferred.

- Minced beef can be used if preferred, but it will have a stronger taste.

- The mince mixture and sauce can also be turned into child-sized portions of lasagne by layering with no-soak pasta sheets. Add a little extra water or stock at the end of cooking, as the lasagne will absorb some of the liquid.

- Passata is sold in jars alongside the other Italian products in the supermarket, but you could use canned chopped tomatoes instead.

Lamb and vegetable casserole

Makes 4–6 servings

- 250g (9oz) lean **lamb fillet**, cubed
- 25g (1oz) unsalted **butter**
- 1 large **carrot**, peeled and diced
- 1 **leek**, washed and thinly sliced
- 300ml (½ pint) home-made **vegetable stock** (page 59) or filtered **water**
- 420g (14oz) can chopped **tomatoes**
- pinch of mixed **dried herbs** or 2 tsp chopped **fresh herbs**

1. Wash the lamb under cold running water and pat dry with kitchen towel.

2. Heat the butter in a casserole dish, and fry lamb until browned all over. Add the carrot and leek and cook for 5 minutes, then add the stock, chopped tomatoes and herbs. Bring to the boil, cover, then lower the heat and simmer for 30–40 minutes.

3. Serve mashed or finely chopped with pasta or rice.

TIPS

- Home-made chicken or vegetable stock (pages 58, 59) could be added instead of tomatoes along with a sprinkling of red lentils or butter beans.

- Many supermarkets sell packs of lean diced lamb but they can be expensive and only available in 450g (1lb) packs. Fillet of lamb is often sold in smaller amounts and is extremely tender.

Pizza potatoes

Makes 4 servings

- 4 small **baking potatoes**, scrubbed
- 100g (3½oz) **mozzarella cheese**, coarsely grated
- 1 **tomato**, skinned and finely chopped
- 1 tsp **tomato purée**
- 1 tbsp finely chopped fresh **basil** (optional)
- 3–4 tbsp organic **full-fat milk**

1. Preheat the oven to 200°C/400°F/gas mark 6. Prick the potatoes and oven bake for 50–60 minutes or until soft.

2. Cut the potatoes in half, scoop out the soft centres and mash on a plate with three-quarters of the cheese, the chopped tomato, the tomato purée, basil (if using) and enough milk to make a creamy mash.

3. Spoon the mixture back into the potato shells. Sprinkle with the remaining cheese. Reheat when needed at the same temperature as in step 1 for 20 minutes until piping hot. Cool to desired temperature for your baby and check before serving.

TIPS

- Don't give potato skins to your baby as they will still be too tricky to chew – they have really only been included here as mini containers.

- As your baby gets more adventurous, try adding other ingredients such as sweetcorn, diced mushrooms or courgettes.

- Adapt the idea to make just one potato as an easy store cupboard supper with whatever mild cheese you may have, plus a few frozen mixed vegetables or frozen well-drained spinach.

Mini salmon skewers

Makes 4 servings

- 350g (12oz) baking **potatoes**, cut into chunks
- 250g (9oz) **butternut squash**, deseeded, peeled and diced
- 250g (9oz) **salmon fillet**, skin removed
- juice of ½ **lime**
- 2 tbsp organic **full-fat milk**
- 15g (½oz) unsalted **butter**
- cooked **broccoli florets**, to serve

1. Half fill the bottom of a two-tier steamer with boiling water, add potatoes to the base and the squash to the top. Cover and steam the squash for 10 minutes, the potatoes for 15 minutes, or until tender.
2. Meanwhile, cut the fish into small squares, carefully checking for and removing any bones. Thread on to 8 wooden cocktail sticks. Squeeze lime juice over and set aside.
3. When the vegetables are cooked, mash the potatoes with the squash, butter and milk until smooth. Keep hot if serving now.
4. Steam the fish for 5 minutes until it is tender and flakes easily. Slide the salmon off the sticks before serving.
5. Serve with just cooked broccoli.

TIPS

- Freeze raw, wrapped in individual portions. Freeze the cooled mash in separate portions.
- As the fish is frozen raw on skewers, make sure to buy fish that hasn't already been frozen first.
- Always *remove* the skewers before serving and *never* leave children unattended while eating.

Mixed vegetable frittata

Makes enough for baby and you

Note: Not suitable for freezing

- 2 tsp **sunflower oil**
- 150g (5oz) cooked **potato**, diced
- 4 tbsp frozen **mixed vegetables**
- 3 **eggs**, beaten
- 1 tbsp freshly grated **Parmesan cheese**
- 1 tbsp organic **full-fat milk**
- 15g (½oz) unsalted **butter**

1. Heat the oil in a small frying pan, add the potato and fry for 4–5 minutes or until golden. Add the frozen vegetables and cook for 2–3 minutes or until softened.

2. Beat the eggs and cheese together with milk. Add the butter to the pan. When melted pour the egg mixture over the vegetables and cook for 3–4 minutes or until the omelette is set and the underside is golden.

3. Preheat the grill to high and cook the top of the omelette for 2–3 minutes until it is golden and the egg mixture is set all the way through. Leave to cool slightly then cut into wedges and serve with cherry tomatoes and cucumber.

TIPS

- This makes a speedy store cupboard supper and is ideal for when you've been out for the day. Perfect for a hungry toddler and his mum.

- Cold frittata also makes good picnic food served in mini pitta breads.

- Eggs are a very concentrated source of cheap protein and are perfectly safe for children as long as they are well cooked.

Chicken-peach casserole

Makes 6–8 servings

- 2 skinless, boneless **chicken breast fillets**, cubed
- 1 tbsp unsalted **butter**
- 1 tbsp **olive oil**
- 1 small **onion**, peeled and chopped
- 2 small **carrots**, peeled and diced
- 1 small **green pepper**, deseeded and chopped
- 8 **cherry tomatoes**, halved
- 150ml (¼ pint) home-made **chicken** or **vegetable stock** (pages 58, 59) or filtered **water**
- 200g (7oz) can sliced **peaches** in natural juice

1. Wash the chicken breasts under cold running water and dry with kitchen towel.
2. Heat the butter and oil in a large frying pan, add the chicken and fry for 3–4 minutes or until brown. Transfer the chicken pieces to a casserole dish.
3. Sweat the onion, carrots and green pepper in the remainder of the oil and butter for approximately 7–8 minutes, then add the tomato halves and the stock, and bring to the boil. Pour the peaches and juice or extra stock or water over the chicken pieces. Cover the casserole and cook for 30 minutes.
4. Serve mashed or finely chopped with rice or pasta.

TIPS

- Rather than canned fruit, use 125g (4oz) ready-to-eat peaches, cut into strips and an extra 150ml (¼ pint) water or stock.
- Serve with easy-cook brown rice or tiny soup pasta for extra texture.

Chinese noodles

Makes enough for baby and you

Note: Not suitable for freezing

- 65g (2½oz) **Chinese egg noodles**
- 2 tsp **sunflower oil**
- 1 small **carrot**, peeled and cut into thin strips
- ¼ **red pepper**, deseeded and cut into strips
- 40g (1½oz) **green beans**, halved lengthways
- 50g (2oz) **pak choi**, well-rinsed and thinly sliced
- 1cm (½in) piece **root ginger**, peeled and coarsely grated
- 1 tbsp **tomato ketchup**
- 4 tbsp boiling filtered **water**

1. Put the noodles into a shallow bowl, cover with boiling water and leave to soak or boil according to packet instructions.
2. Heat the oil in a wok or frying pan, add the carrot, red pepper and green bean strips and stir-fry for 3 minutes. Add the pak choi, ginger, ketchup and water and stir-fry for 2 minutes. Add the drained noodles, heat through and serve.

TIPS

- Delicious served topped with a thin egg omelette, rolled up like a Swiss roll and cut into thin strips.
- Beansprouts can be used in place of the pak choi.

Chicken with sweet peppers

Makes 2–3 servings

- 1 tbsp **olive oil**
- ¼ small **red onion**, finely sliced
- ½ **garlic** clove, crushed
- 1 **chicken breast fillet**, skinned, boned and cubed
- 200g (7oz) can chopped **tomatoes**
- ½ **red pepper**, chopped
- pinch of **mixed dried herbs** or 2 tsp finely chopped **fresh herbs**

1. Heat the oil in a saucepan, add the onion and crushed garlic, and sweat for 2–3 minutes.
2. Add the cubed chicken breast and fry in the oil for 1–2 minutes or until browned all over.
3. Add the tomatoes, peppers and herbs. Bring to the boil, then lower the heat and simmer, uncovered, for approximately 10–15 minutes.
4. Serve with rice or pasta.

TIPS

- Diced courgettes or mushrooms, or both, could also be added in place of the peppers.
- As your baby progresses to lumpier, coarser textures you may also like to serve this with soaked couscous or tiny cooked soup pasta.

Chicken and butter bean burgers

Makes 4 servings

Note: Only the burgers can be frozen

- 175g (6oz) minced **chicken**
- 100g (3½oz) canned **butter beans** (without salt or sugar) or **home-cooked beans**, drained
- 2 **spring onions**, roughly chopped
- **plain flour**, for shaping

To serve:

- 4 small soft **bread rolls**
- a little **tomato ketchup**
- a little shredded **lettuce**
- 1 **tomato**, thinly sliced

1. Put the chicken, beans and spring onions into a blender or food processor and blend together.
2. Shape into four small rounds with wet or floured hands. Wrap each burger in cling film, if freezing.
3. Preheat the grill to high. Cook burgers for 8 minutes, turning once or twice until they are browned and cooked through and the juices run clear when pierced with a knife. Cut one of the burgers in half, to make doubly sure they are cooked before serving.
4. Split the bread rolls, toast if liked and then spread one side with ketchup, add lettuce and tomato and top with a hot burger.

TIPS

- If your local supermarket doesn't sell ready-minced chicken, then buy the same weight of boneless, skinless chicken breast fillets and finely chop in a blender or food processor.

- For children who are not salad fans, leave the tomato and lettuce out of the bun and serve with carrot and cucumber sticks or slices of apple instead.

- Mixing the chicken with butter beans is a good way of introducing vegetable protein and fibre into your child's diet.

Chicken and mushroom stir-fry

Makes 2–3 servings

- 1 **chicken breast fillet**, skinned and boned
- 1 tsp **plain flour**
- 1 tsp **low-salt soy sauce**
- 2 tsp **vegetable oil**
- ¼ small **onion**, finely sliced
- ½ **garlic** clove, crushed
- 25g (1oz) **button mushrooms**, chopped

1. Cube the chicken into bite-sized pieces. Place in a bowl and coat with the flour, sprinkle with the soy sauce and leave for 15 minutes.

2. Heat the oil in wok or frying pan, add the chicken and stir-fry for 2–3 minutes. Lower the heat and push the chicken to one side, then add the onion and crushed garlic, if using. Cook for a further 2–3 minutes. Finally, mix in the mushrooms and stir-fry for a further 1–2 minutes.

3. Serve with pasta or rice.

TIPS

- Look out for low-salt versions of soy sauce if you can.

- Vary the vegetables depending on what you have in the salad drawer, add strips of carrot, courgette, green beans, mangetout or red pepper if available.

Beef and lentil pot supper

Makes 4–6 servings

- 300g (10oz) lean **minced beef**
- 1 small **onion**, finely chopped
- 2 tsp **olive oil**
- 225g (8oz) **carrot**, peeled and diced
- 150g (5oz) **swede**, peeled and diced
- 75g (3oz) **red lentils**, rinsed
- 900ml (1½ pints) home-made **chicken** or **vegetable stock** (pages 58, 59) or filtered **water**
- 1 tbsp **tomato purée**
- 1 **bouquet garni**, fresh or dried

1. Preheat the oven to 180°C/350°F/gas mark 4.
2. Fry the mince and onion in oil in a flameproof casserole or frying pan, stirring until browned.
3. Add the remaining ingredients and bring to the boil, stirring. Transfer to a casserole dish if not using a flameproof casserole dish. Cover and cook for 1½ hours or until the lentils and vegetables are tender.
4. Remove the bouquet garni. Finely chop or mash the beef and lentils as needed.

TIPS

- This mixture can also be spooned into individual ovenproof dishes and topped with mashed potato, shepherd's pie style.
- For adventurous babies add a little crushed garlic.

Chicken and vegetable oat crumble

Makes 4–6 servings

- 2 tbsp **olive oil**
- 2 **chicken breast fillets**, skinned and boned
- ½ small **onion**, diced
- 1 tbsp **plain flour**
- 300ml (½ pint) home-made **chicken** or **vegetable stock** (pages 58, 59) or filtered **water**
- 200g (7oz) **carrots**, diced
- 200g (7oz) **swede**, diced
- 100g (3½oz) **courgettes**, diced
- 2 sticks **celery**, diced

Topping:

- 5 tbsp fresh **wholemeal breadcrumbs**
- 5 tbsp **porridge oats**
- 5 tbsp grated mild **Cheddar cheese**

1. Preheat the oven to 200°C/400°F/gas mark 6.
2. Heat the oil in a large saucepan, add the chicken and onion and fry until the chicken is sealed. Add the flour and cook for 1–2 minutes.
3. Gradually stir in the stock and cook over a low heat until it begins to thicken, then stir in the vegetables. Bring to the boil, then cover, lower the heat and simmer for 10–15 minutes or until the vegetables are just tender.
4. Meanwhile, mix together the topping ingredients and set aside.
5. Spoon the chicken and vegetable mixture into an ovenproof dish. Sprinkle over the topping ingredients and bake for 20–25 minutes or until the top is golden brown.
6. Serve mashed or finely chopped.

TIPS

- Adding a crunchy gratin-style topping is a good way to introduce texture to your baby's meals.

- If your child is naturally cutting down on milk, it can be helpful to know that just 40g (1½oz) of Cheddar cheese is equivalent to 200ml (7floz) of full-fat milk.

Kiddies' kedgeree

Makes 4 servings

- 2 tsp **olive oil**

- 1 small **onion**, finely chopped

- 100g (3½oz) **easy-cook long grain brown rice**, rinsed

- a large pinch of **ground turmeric**

- ¼ tsp **garam masala**

- 750ml (1¼ pints) home-made **vegetable stock** (page 59) or filtered **water**

- 2 **eggs**

- 75g (3oz) frozen **mixed vegetables**

- 200g (7oz) can **tuna** in spring water, well-drained and flaked

1. Heat the oil in a saucepan, add the onion and fry for 5 minutes or until soft. Stir in the rice and spices and cook for 1 minute.

2. Pour on the stock, bring to the boil, then cover, lower the heat and simmer for 30 minutes or until the rice is tender .

3. Meanwhile, put the eggs in a small saucepan and cover with cold water. Bring to the boil, cover, then lower the heat and simmer for 8 minutes or until hard-boiled. Drain. Peel the eggs and chop finely.

4. Add the vegetables, tuna and eggs to the rice. Spoon into the dishes, coarsely mashing or finely chopping to suit your baby.

TIPS

- Hard-boiled egg freezes well if very finely chopped.

- Brown rice contains more vitamins and minerals than white, but the phytic acid in the bran inhibits the absorption of iron and calcium. Easy-cook brown rice has some of the bran removed, making it a better alternative for young children.

Baby Bolognese

Makes 4–6 servings

- 150g (5oz) extra-lean **minced beef steak**
- 1 small **onion**, peeled and finely chopped
- 75g (3oz) **button mushrooms**, wiped and sliced
- 200g (7oz) **carrots**, peeled and diced
- 150g (5oz) **courgettes**, diced
- a few stems of fresh **marjoram** or large pinch of dried marjoram
- **oil** for frying
- 600ml (1 pint) home-made **chicken stock** (page 58) or boiling filtered **water**
- 75g (3oz) **soup pasta**
- 2 tsp **tomato purée** (optional)

1. Dry-fry the meat and onion together in a saucepan until browned. Stir-fry the other vegetables with a little oil. Remove from the heat and add the herbs and stock or water. Return to the heat, cover and bring to the boil, then lower the heat and simmer for 30 minutes, stirring occasionally, until beef and vegetables are tender.

2. Meanwhile, cook pasta in a saucepan of boiling water for 6–7 minutes (or according to the packet instructions) or until tender. Drain well.

3. Purée the beef and pasta together in a blender, in batches if necessary. Mix in the tomato purée, if using.

TIPS

*   As beef has a strong taste, use slightly less than other meats until your baby is happy with this new flavour.

*   When your baby is older, adapt this dinner by puréeing the meat mixture and mixing with chopped pasta to introduce him to coarser, more textured dishes.

Pick-up sticks
Makes enough for baby and you
Note: Not suitable for freezing

*   1 small ripe **avocado**
*   juice of ½ **lime**
*   1 tbsp organic **full-fat milk**
*   1 tsp chopped fresh **coriander leaves** (optional)
*   2 **pitta breads**
*   selection **carrot**, **cucumber** and **celery** sticks

1. Mash the avocado with the lime juice and milk, add coriander, if using, and spoon the mixture into two small plastic dishes.
2. Preheat the grill to high. Sprinkle pitta bread with water and grill for 2–3 minutes. Leave to cool, then cut into strips and serve with veggy sticks and pots of avocado mixture.

TIPS

*   Avocados are a powerhouse of concentrated energy – ideal for busy toddlers with small appetites.

*   This kind of food is not only quick and easy to prepare but good to share with adults, too.

5 Twelve months and over

By the age of 12 months your baby should be eating three meals a day and drinking all or most of his milk feeds from a beaker. He now needs a minimum of 350ml (12oz) a day and a maximum of 600ml (20oz), divided between two and three milk feeds and inclusive of milk used in cereal and cooking. Failure to discard the bottle after one year can lead many babies to drink well in excess of their daily requirements, which can make them very fussy about eating solids, and may even cause iron deficiency anaemia, as cow's milk is low in iron.

During the second year a child's growth slows down and there is often a decrease in appetite. I have quoted Elizabeth Morse, author of *My Child Won't Eat,* to hundreds of anxious parents who are worried about their child's eating habits. She says, 'If a child continued to grow at the same rate as in the first year, he would be 29 metres long and weigh 200 tonnes by the age of ten.' In my experience parents are often not made aware of this fact, and are unrealistic as to what their child really needs for a healthy and well-balanced diet during the second year. Constant pressure on the child to eat can lead to mealtimes becoming a real battle of wills, creating long-term feeding problems.

If your baby does become very fussy during his second year and you are concerned that he is developing a feeding problem it might be a good idea to keep a food diary for at least one week. Some toddlers will eat very little for two or three days, then eat an enormous amount the following day. Refer to pages 6–8 on what your baby needs to eat for a healthy and well-balanced diet. For example, he needs 3–4 servings of carbohydrates a day, made up of cereal, bread, pasta or potatoes. It is very possible that your food diary will show a pattern where he is only eating one or two servings some days but has five or six on other days. This is perfectly normal and it is important to look at your child's food intake over several days, not the amount he eats in a single day. I have not included a feeding plan or recipes in this section, because once your baby is over a year old he should be eating a wide and varied range of meals, joining in most, if not all, of the family meals. Always remember, though, not to add salt until the baby's portion has been served.

The following guidelines should help you establish good eating habits for your toddler and hopefully help you to avoid serious eating problems.

Feeding guidelines

- If you wish to prevent your baby becoming a fussy feeder and a toddler who refuses healthy food, it is important to continue structuring his milk feeding so that the problem of excessive milk intake does not occur. He needs a minimum of 350ml (12oz) a day, divided between two and three milk feeds and inclusive of milk used in cooking and on cereal.

- Some toddlers will actually start to refuse their milk during the second year. If your toddler is taking less than the required minimum, try to increase the amount used on cereals and in sauces and healthy puddings. Include additional servings of yoghurt, fromage frais, cheese and dark green leafy vegetables, which are high in calcium.

- Good eating habits can be encouraged at this stage by introducing a wide variety of different tastes and textures and varying the way you prepare and serve his meals. Offer small quantities of different foods rather than large amounts of one or two foods. As your baby becomes more aware of different colours and shapes, try to make food look attractive. A selection of two or three different-coloured vegetables served with his chicken or fish at lunchtime will be much more appealing than the different foods still being mixed up altogether.

• Fruit juice can also take the edge off a toddler's appetite. Try to encourage water in between meals; if fruit juice is given it should be very well diluted and offered no later than two hours before his meal. At mealtimes it is best to give your toddler at least half his food before offering water or juice – allowing drinks just before a meal may really affect his appetite.

• Look at the times you are feeding your toddler – an over-tired or over-hungry child will not eat well. Try to ensure that breakfast is finished by 8am, so that he is ready for lunch around 12 noon. This should ensure that he is ready for a good tea at 5pm.

• Avoid giving snacks or drinks too close to mealtimes as they can take the edge off his appetite. Try to give mid-morning snacks and drinks around 9.30/10am and mid-afternoon snacks and drinks no later than 3pm.

• Try to stick to regular mealtimes and avoid distractions such as television or playing games. Avoid cajoling, forcing or bribing your toddler with puddings or sweets as an incentive to eat as this is one of the surest ways of creating a long-term eating problem. If your child starts to mess around with his food or become fussy, remove the food without making any comment about him not eating. Try then to make him wait until his next scheduled meal or snack before giving him anything to eat or drink.

• Sugar is another cause of loss of appetite and levels can be quite high in many commercial foods such as baked beans, tinned soups, fruits, etc. Some leading brands of fromage frais have as much as 14.5g (½oz) of sugar in a 100g (3½oz) pot. Always check the label for the list of ingredients and avoid food with high levels of sugar, starches and fillers, all of which can reduce a toddler's appetite for healthy food.

- Most babies can eat the same foods as the rest of the family as long as they are cut into bite-sized pieces. Encouraging your baby to self-feed at this stage also plays a very important part in establishing good feeding habits. Try to avoid being over-fussy about how messy meals have become. The important thing is that your baby feels happy and relaxed at mealtimes and is attempting to get the food into his mouth, even if it is mostly by using his fingers.

Davina: aged 18 months

Davina first started to refuse milk when she was 14 months old. By the time she was 18 months old she was drinking no milk at all, although she would take milk on her breakfast cereal. Davina's parents sought medical advice from both the health visitor and local GP. They were advised to give her lots of cheese and yoghurt, as well as milk on cereal, to compensate for her refusal to drink milk. The reason they contacted me was that they were very worried about Davina's other fluid intake, which amounted to approximately 180–240ml (6–8oz) a day. They were also worried about the fact that she was still eating jars of baby food, was eating a very limited range of foods and that each meal was becoming a battle of wills, with her refusing to be spoon-fed. They would dance, sing and cajole her into eating, often resorting to force-feeding her.

I advised Davina's parents to keep a very detailed food diary of everything she ate and drank, also the exact amounts consumed and the times she ate. Once I received this it was clear that much of the problem was being caused by her snacks in between meals and the jars of food. Davina's food diary consisted of the following:

Breakfast: 8.20am

1 Weetabix with milk and chopped fruit

3 mini bix

¼ slice of toast with butter and Marmite

60ml (2oz) water

Lunch: 12.40pm

1 large jar of organic baby food, eaten with great reluctance

1 large yoghurt

½ slice of bread and butter

1 dessertspoon of flaked fish

½ Baby Bel cheese

30ml (1oz) water

3.30pm

1 slice of ginger cake

½ slice of bread and butter

Tea: 6pm

1 large jar of organic baby food

1 large yoghurt

1 tablespoon of peas and sweetcorn

1 tablespoon of mixed bean salad

1 slice cucumber

¼ croissant

60ml (2oz) water

3 mini bix

As Davina was becoming very difficult about eating from the spoon, I advised her parents to cut out her mini bix and reduce her amount of Weetabix in the morning so that she took all her yoghurt and fruit requirements first thing in the morning when she was really hungry. This had the knock-on effect of making her hungrier at lunchtime. We stopped the jars altogether and offered her a selection of cold cuts of very thinly sliced meats or fish, and finger food vegetables at lunchtime so that she could be in control of her feeding. Within two days she was actually taking all her protein and vegetable requirements at lunch so that we could be more relaxed about tea. We stopped giving her cake and bread mid-afternoon and replaced it with a small piece of fresh fruit, which made her hungry for her tea. Then at teatime we offered her a selection of finger food vegetables and salad, with cheese and bread, followed by either carrot or banana cake. By the end of the week her food diary showed that all her food requirements were being met and, even better, she trebled her fluid intake.

Your questions answered

Q　My toddler's eating habits have become very erratic over the last few months. Some days he will eat three good meals a day, on other days just one, and some days he just snacks all day. How do I get him back to eating three good meals a day?

A　• This erratic eating pattern is very common during a child's second and third year and, as long as he is eating healthy food, it is better to go with it. In my experience children who are cajoled, bribed or forced to eat usually end up

with long-term eating problems. However, it is important
to set some rules and boundaries about eating to ensure
that your child's nutritional needs are met with a variety of
healthy foods over a period of several days.

• Allow a certain length of time for meals. If your child is
fussing and refusing food after this time, don't make any
comment, simply remove the meal and make him wait for
any further food until his next snack or meal is due.

• Keep a food diary, listing all the foods and drinks your
child consumes and at what times. Make a note of his
behaviour at mealtimes and whether you think his lack of
appetite could have been caused by overtiredness or
getting overexcited.

• Pay very close attention to the timing and type of snacks
you are giving. Snacks and drinks should always be given
midway between meals – giving them too close to a meal
can take the edge off a toddler's appetite. It is also
important to select healthy snacks that are not too filling
– fresh and dried fruit or raw chopped vegetables are
preferable to more filling foods such as cheese,
breadsticks or biscuits. Try to avoid things like sweets, ice
creams and crisps as they are of little nutritional value
and will fill your toddler up with empty calories.

• Excessive milk intake is another cause of toddlers not
eating well at mealtimes. Your toddler needs a minimum
of 350ml (12oz) and a maximum of 600ml (20oz) of full-
fat milk a day. These amounts are best given as a drink
first thing in the morning and on breakfast cereal and as a
drink last thing at night, with the remainder used in
cooking. Milk given as a drink between meals can really
take the edge off the appetite.

Q   **My toddler is eating a wide variety of carbohydrates,
such as bread, pasta and potatoes, plus lots of fruit and**

vegetables, as finger foods, but I am having real problems
getting him to eat meat or fish.

A   • Many toddlers do refuse to eat meat at this age. Try
       offering very thinly cut slices of chicken, turkey, lamb or
       beef spread with a little Marmite. Good-quality meat or
       vegetarian sausages are also worth trying. The important
       thing is not to force your toddler to eat something he
       clearly dislikes. There are many vegetarian alternatives that
       can provide him with all his protein needs.

     • Offering your toddler plenty of pulses, e.g. lentils and
       chick peas, plus cheese, yoghurt, soya and eggs with his
       other foods will ensure that he receives enough protein. It
       is also worthwhile investing in a couple of recipe books
       that specialise in vegetarian cookery for children to make
       sure you fully understand how to combine vegetable
       proteins so that your toddler receives a nutritionally
       balanced diet.

Q   My toddler has suddenly taken a real dislike to his milk
     and is now taking a lot less than 350ml (12oz) a day. Some
     nights he flatly refuses his bedtime drink.

A   • Babies and young toddlers are not capable of
       distinguishing between hunger and thirst, and therefore it
       would be wise to check that your toddler is not eating too
       much solid food at mealtimes, which could have a knock-
       on effect on the amount of milk he is drinking. For several
       days keep a note of all the food, milk and other fluids that
       he consumes over each 24-hour period and the times he
       consumes them. Check on pages 128–30 for guidelines on
       how much a toddler needs to eat at this age. If the amounts
       he is eating over several days seem well in excess of the

guidelines, gradually cut back on his solids to see if this
helps increase the amount of milk he wants.

• When toddlers refuse milk at this age it is sometimes
because they have drunk too much water or juice in the
late afternoon, which then affects their bedtime bottle.
Try to offer your child a mid-afternoon drink of water
only no later than 3pm, and offer only a couple of ounces
of fluids with his tea.

• Record details of the times he does drink milk and the
amounts he consumes. Gradually reduce his milk intake
during the day to see if he will increase the amount he
takes at bedtime.

• If your toddler still refuses his milk offer him a yoghurt at
both breakfast and lunch, and include a serving of cheese
in his daily diet. Also try to include lots of sauces and
milk puddings in his diet and milk-shake drinks made
with fruit and fromage frais or yoghurt.

Feeding the Family

Once your baby has been introduced to a wide range of foods and
is happily eating three meals a day it is advisable that you start to
include him in family meals, particularly if you have a toddler or
older children to cook for as well. This will not only reduce the
number of hours you spend cooking different meals, but will also
help your baby establish healthy eating habits and good social skills
at mealtimes.

Babies and toddlers learn by example, and family mealtimes give
you the perfect opportunity to teach your baby and toddler about
saying please and thank you, and how to use their cutlery properly
and feed themselves.

As your baby nears the end of his first year it is important to
realise that he is becoming more independent and will develop likes
and dislikes to certain foods. It is important not to get into a battle
of wills with him regarding food. Offer him a variety and try not

to force him to eat certain foods if he refuses them. Leave them out of his diet for a couple of weeks and then re-introduce them. More likely than not he will accept the food he so stubbornly refused previously. Cooking a huge batch of special meals for your baby and having them totally rejected can be quite upsetting. By including your baby and toddler in as many family meals as possible it enables you to offer him a variety of different foods at each meal, without getting stressed if he refuses them.

For ideas on creating meals that the whole family can enjoy, you can refer to my cook book, *The Gina Ford Baby and Toddler Cook Book*. There you'll find recipes that are suited to the needs of a family trying to feed differently-aged children as well as their parents. There are quick and easy recipes for a weekday supper, weekday lunches after nursery and/or pre-school, family meals at the weekend, as well as ideas for baking, puddings and birthday party food. All the recipes can be adapted for the whole family.

One important thing to note when you are cooking for the whole family is to remember not to use salt or pepper. When serving, remove the children's portions then add seasoning to the rest.

6 A–Z of Foods

Apples (first stage food)

Apples are an ideal first weaning food but need to be cooked and puréed until your baby is between six and seven months of age. They can then be given raw, but should still be peeled and puréed or grated. Between nine and 12 months, the majority of babies are able to chew small pieces of soft peeled apple.

Health benefits

Apples are reported to help reduce cholesterol levels and contain cancer-fighting agents. They are high in soluble fibre, which can help prevent constipation when eaten raw. They are also a good source of vitamin C and bioflavonoids. Note that the vitamin C content varies considerably, depending on the variety of apple.

Buying and storing

Choose eating apples that are firm, brightly coloured and without blemishes. To keep them moist and crisp, remove any plastic wrapping and store the fruit at a cool temperature or in the refrigerator.

Preparation

To prevent the apple turning brown do not peel or slice it until you are ready to cook it. It should then be peeled, quartered, cored, covered with a small amount of freshly filtered water, and cooked as soon as possible.

Cooking

Add just enough freshly filtered boiling water to cover, then put a lid on the pan, lower the heat and simmer until soft. Remove the apple from the water and purée to a smooth texture in a blender, adding some of the cooking liquid to get the desired consistency. When cool, the required amount should be given to your baby immediately, and any leftovers put in a suitable container and stored in the refrigerator.

Apricots (from seven months)

Fresh apricots are best introduced at around seven months, when they can be given raw. Dried apricots can also be given from seven months onwards, but would need to be cooked and puréed until your baby is around one year old and able to chew them properly.

Health benefits

Fresh and dried apricots are very rich in antioxidants, particularly beta carotene. Dried apricots, in particular, are an excellent source of iron, are high in fibre and a good source of potassium. They are said to offer some protection against cancer and respiratory infections, and may help to regulate blood pressure.

Buying and storing

Choose fresh apricots with firm smooth skins that are blemish-free. Hard, under-ripe fruits should be avoided, as they tend to have a sour taste. Apricots should be stored in the refrigerator and used within 2–3 days.

Preparation

Although fresh apricots can be served raw, either mashed or puréed, from seven months, it is advisable to remove the skins. Wash them in a colander under cold running water, then cover with filtered, boiled water for approximately one minute, then for one minute with cold water to loosen the skins. Peel away the skins, and cut the fruits in quarters to remove the stone and pith. Purée to a smooth texture using a blender or mash finely with a fork. If necessary a small amount of cool, freshly filtered boiled water can be used to get the desired consistency. Dried stoneless apricots should be washed in a colander under cold running water and placed in a pan with enough fresh filtered water to cover.

Cooking

Bring the fruit to the boil, cover with a lid and simmer until tender. Drain the fruit and purée to a smooth texture in a blender. If necessary use the reserved liquid to adjust the purée to the desired consistency.

Asparagus (from seven months)

Asparagus can be introduced in cooking from seven months, but it is best used as a finger food when your baby is getting towards a year old.

Health benefits

Asparagus is an excellent source of the antioxidants glutathione and beta carotene, which may help to prevent certain cancers. It is a good source of the vitamins A and C. Asparagus is also reported to have sedative qualities and can act as a mild diuretic.

Buying and storing

Choose firm and fresh-looking stalks. Whether they are green or white depends on the variety rather than the quality, but avoid any that look droopy or have thin, wrinkled or woody stems. Since asparagus needs to be eaten really fresh, the further it has travelled, the less likely it is to be the best quality. Asparagus should be kept in the bottom of the fridge with other perishable vegetables.

Preparation

Rinse each stalk gently and break or cut off the end if it is tough and woody. Scrape or shave the lengths of each stalk, starting just below the tip. Trim the stalks to roughly the same lengths and then tie them in bundles of 6–8 stalks for steaming, tying them under the tips and near the base of the stalks.

Cooking
Wedge the bundles, tips facing upwards, in a deep saucepan with enough filtered boiling water to come three-quarters of the way up the stalks. Cover the tips with a cap of foil and simmer gently until tender. This means the stalks are boiled and the delicate tips are steamed. Very fresh asparagus will need to cook for only 3–5 minutes, otherwise for about 10 minutes. Drain well on kitchen towel and freshen under cold water, then drain and serve either mashed or chopped.

Aubergine (from nine to twelve months)
This can be popular when stuffed with layers of cheese and tomato and then roasted. It is a great vegetable to add to dishes like moussaka.

Health benefits
Aubergines are not reported to have any particular health benefits, apart from being low in fat and sodium. They contain a small amount of the vitamin B_2 and medium amounts of vitamin B_1 and potassium.

Buying and storing
Choose firm, smooth aubergines with dark shiny blemish-free skins. Aubergines can be kept for 5–7 days if refrigerated.

Preparation
To prevent aubergines turning brown they should not be cut until they are ready to be cooked. Wash under cold running water and dry with kitchen towel.

Cooking

Aubergines are best used in dishes such as moussaka and other savoury bakes.

Avocado (first stage food)

Avocado is often recommended as an early weaning food. However, because of its high fat content I prefer to wait until the second part of the first stage before introducing it. I have found that many babies take longer to digest it than the very first weaning foods, causing them to cut back too much on the following milk feed.

Health benefits

Avocado is an excellent source of vitamin E, and provides reasonable amounts of vitamins A, B and C. It is also a good source of potassium and protein. It has a high level of monounsaturated fat which is believed to help lower blood cholesterol levels, and some experts believe it can also help prevent clogging of the arteries.

Buying and storing

Choose avocados with smooth, shiny bright green blemish-free skins, as they tend to be sweeter than the dark green or purple-coloured ones. The avocado is ripe if the ends of the fruit feel soft when pressed. Ripe avocados are best stored at a cool temperature or in the refrigerator, where they should keep for 3–4 days. Avocados cannot be frozen.

Preparation

Wash under cold running water, cut in half and remove the stone. Scoop the flesh from one half and mash to a smooth texture using a fork. If necessary the consistency can be adjusted by mixing in a small amount of formula, expressed milk or cool freshly boiled water. The remaining half of the fruit should be brushed with lemon juice, wrapped tightly in foil and stored immediately in the refrigerator.

Cooking

Avocados require no cooking and are best served in salads or mashed as dips.

Bananas (from six months)

Highly recommended as a first weaning food. However, I prefer to introduce them later because I have found that bananas mixed with baby rice can cause constipation and digestive problems for many babies under six months old.

Health benefits

Bananas are high in the mineral potassium, which is essential for good muscle and nerve function and regulating blood pressure. They are also said to be effective in treating stomach upsets and diarrhoea, especially when served with rice and cooked apples. Because bananas are very high in natural sugars, they are believed to be very effective in raising energy levels.

Buying and storing

Choose creamy yellow-coloured bananas with smooth blemish-free skins. Allow two or three days for them to ripen; once they have developed brown spots on their skins they are ready to eat. If the fruit has touches of green on it, it will need longer to ripen and should not be used as it can cause severe indigestion in young babies. Bananas should be stored at room temperature, not in the refrigerator. Bananas cannot be frozen.

Preparation

Bananas require no cooking and should not be cut or peeled until they are ready to be eaten as they very quickly turn brown. When required, peel and mash half a banana to a smooth texture with a fork, using formula, breast milk or cool, freshly boiled water.

Beans see Green beans and Pulses

Beansprouts (from one year)

These can be a great finger food to give alongside any dish, but are best served in a salad.

Health benefits

Beansprouts are not renowned for having any particular health benefits but they are a good source of vitamin C, and provide medium amounts of the B vitamins and the mineral potassium.

Buying and storing

Choose crisp, small, fresh shoots or grow them yourself at home. Beansprouts take only 4–7 days to sprout from mung beans. Beansprouts should be kept in the bottom of the fridge with other salad and perishable vegetables.

Preparation

Rinse in filtered water.

Cooking

Cook as soon as possible after buying or harvesting. Either blanch for 30 seconds in filtered boiling water or stir-fry for 1–2 minutes. Serve hot as an accompaniment, cold as part of a salad or stir-fried with other vegetable ingredients and meat or chicken.

Beef (from nine to twelve months)

I have found that beef is best introduced when your baby is able to eat mince without it being puréed. I always find that a simple cottage pie or lasagne is popular.

Health benefits
Beef is high in protein and an excellent source of vitamins and minerals, particularly the B vitamins and iron and zinc.

Buying and storing
Choose good-quality organic beef – the leanest cuts are rump or fillet. It is important to remove beef from the plastic packaging it is bought in, particularly if it is not going to be cooked on the day of purchase. All beef should be washed under cold running water, and dried with kitchen towel before being stored in the coldest part of the refrigerator. Once cleaned, it should be placed on a clean plate and loosely covered with foil.

It is very important to keep raw meat separate from cooked meat. Store raw meat in the coldest part of the refrigerator.

Preparation
Trim the beef carefully, cutting away all the visible fat.

Cooking
Less-tender cuts need added liquid and longer slower cooking; methods here include braising, pot roasting, stewing and boiling. The tender cuts of meat are best cooked quickly by dry heat, either roasting, grilling or dry-frying.

Beetroot (from nine to twelve months)
Although it is possible to purée beetroot, I have never found it to be very popular with babies, and usually wait until the baby is taking mashed or diced food before introducing it.

Health benefits
Beetroot is an excellent source of potassium and folic acid. It is also believed to offer protection against some cancers.

Buying and storing

Choose small, firm smooth beets with blemish-free skins. Like potatoes and turnips they are best stored in a cool dark airy cupboard,
where they should keep for about two months. If stored at room
temperature they would need to be used within a week.

Preparation

Wash the beets under cold running water, taking care not to break
the skin. Trim slightly the tops and roots.

Cooking

Put the beets in a large pan with plenty of freshly filtered water. Bring
to the boil, cover and simmer until tender. Drain and carefully remove
the skins by rubbing. They can then be mashed or diced as and when
needed. Any remaining beets can be stored in the refrigerator.

Berries (from nine to twelve months)

Although blackberries, blackcurrants, blueberries, cranberries, etc.,
can be introduced sooner than nine months in a purée, they are so
fiddly to prepare that I usually wait until the baby is well established on finger foods, and introduce them raw at that stage.

Health benefits

All berries are a good source of vitamin C and can help improve
iron absorption when eaten alongside non-meat sources of iron,
e.g. breakfast cereals. However, they may cause allergies in children
from allergic families, so should be introduced with care into the
diet of such babies.

Buying and storing

Choose plump, fresh and firm-looking fruit that is stored in containers with no signs of leaking. Fruit that is leaking is potentially
mouldy. Berries should be loosely covered in brown paper bags,
kept in the refrigerator and used within 2–3 days.

Preparation

Wash the berries in a colander under cold running water. Remove stems and leaves and any crushed fruit. Check for grubs when doing this, particularly with fruit that already has stems missing.

Cooking

Berries can be given whole to babies over nine months old who have mastered eating several finger foods. For babies who are still learning to eat finger foods the berries should be puréed to a smooth texture then put through a sieve to remove the skins and seeds.

Bread (between six and seven months)

Once you are confident that your baby can tolerate wheat (in breakfast cereal and pasta) then you can introduce him to bread. The easiest way is first to introduce it as breadcrumbs used as a topping on vegetable or fish pies. As your baby's chewing develops and he shows signs of wanting to feed himself he will enjoy small bite-sized pieces of buttered toast, particularly when he starts teething.

Health benefits

Bread is a good source of carbohydrate and starch. Wholemeal bread has a higher fibre content than white, but all bread is a good source of B vitamins.

Buying and storing

Choose an organic wholemeal loaf which is free of whole grains of any sort. Bread is best stored in a separate bread bin where the air is able to circulate, and it should stay fresh for 3–4 days.

Preparation

Introduce bread as a topping on cooked dishes. Cut off the crusts and place the bread in a food processor for a few moments until it has turned to very fine breadcrumbs. Depending on the recipe, it can be mixed with a variety of different foods, such as cheese and oats to form a nutritious topping on vegetable bakes, fish pies and meat casseroles, etc.

Once your baby is capable of self-feeding he can be offered small pieces of toast with butter and miniature sandwiches with different spreads on. Breadsticks are also very popular with babies who are used to finger foods.

Broccoli (between six and seven months)

Once your baby is eating a variety of root vegetables and the blander green vegetables, you can try introducing broccoli. By starting off with very small amounts – say, one tablespoonful of broccoli mixed with 2–3 tablespoonfuls of sweet potato plus 1–2 tablespoonfuls of carrot, your baby will be less likely to reject the broccoli.

Health benefits
Broccoli is rich in antioxidants and believed to help protect against cancer, particularly cancer of the lungs and breast. It is a good source of vitamin C and contains useful amounts of potassium and folic acid.

Buying and storing
Choose dark-coloured, fresh-looking broccoli with firm stalks and tightly closed heads. It should be stored in the refrigerator and used within 2–3 days.

Preparation
Rinse under cold running water then soak in salted water for 30 minutes to get rid of any insects. Trim the stalks, removing the leaves, and break into even-sized florets. It then needs to be washed several times under cold running water to remove the salt.

Cooking

Place florets in a pan and cover with cold filtered water. Bring to the boil, then lower the heat and simmer, uncovered, until tender. Remove from cooking liquid and purée to a smooth texture using a blender. Any remaining cooking liquid can be used to get the right consistency.

Brussels sprouts (from eight to nine months)

Brussels sprouts can cause quite severe wind in young babies so I rarely introduce them before eight months. If your baby is happy taking other green vegetables, such as cabbage or broccoli, with no side effects, now is the time to try Brussels sprouts.

Health benefits

Brussels sprouts are high in antioxidants and other cancer-fighting agents which may be of help in preventing cancer of the colon and stomach.

Buying and storing

Choose small, firm sprouts with fresh-looking and compact, brightly coloured green leaves. Store as for asparagus.

Preparation

The sprouts should be plunged into cold salted water to get rid of any insects. They should then be trimmed and a cross cut in the base of the sprout. Finally, they should be washed thoroughly in a colander under cold running water.

Cooking

Put the sprouts in a pan and cover with just enough freshly filtered boiled water, then lower the heat and simmer, uncovered, until the sprouts are tender. Drain off the water, and either chop the sprouts roughly or cut into bite-sized pieces, depending on how well your baby is at chewing at this stage. A small knob of butter will enhance their flavour.

Butter (between six and seven months)

Initially I would only use small amounts of butter in cooking. Once finger foods are established it is excellent on bread or toast.

Health benefits

Butter is a good source of vitamins A and D. However, it is also high in saturated fat and calories, so use it in moderation.

Buying and storing

Use unsalted butter for children. Butter is also perfect for freezing for up to six months. Defrost thoroughly before using.

Preparation

When used for cooking, butter is a natural product and gives good flavour to baking. Store butter in the fridge or in a cool dark place, well wrapped or covered to prevent it from absorbing other flavours. Butter will keep for 2–3 weeks (or until the 'best before' date on the package).

Cooking

Remove butter from the fridge at least one hour before cooking to allow it to soften.

Cabbage (from seven to eight months)

Cabbage is another vegetable that can cause problems with wind in some babies. Your baby will be more likely to accept the cabbage if it is introduced in small amounts, and mixed with 2–3 tablespoonfuls of creamed potato.

When your baby is between nine and 12 months old and eating a wide variety of chopped and cubed food, you can try offering him a small amount of very finely chopped cabbage.

Health benefits

Cabbage is high in vitamin C and is believed to contain antioxidants that may help prevent cancer of the colon.

Buying and storing

Choose cabbages with tightly closed leaves that look fresh and crisp and feel heavy for their size. Cabbages should be stored loosely in a paper bag in the refrigerator and used within 5–7 days.

Preparation

Wash cabbage leaves under a cold running tap and break into small pieces.

Cooking

Put the cabbage leaves in a pan and cover with a very small amount of filtered water. Bring to the boil, then lower the heat and simmer, uncovered, until tender. Remove from the cooking liquid and purée to a very smooth texture in a blender. Any remaining cooking liquid can be used to get the right consistency. Alternatively a knob of butter can be added.

Carrots (first stage food)

Carrots are one of the most popular weaning foods, loved by the majority of babies. However, keep a watchful eye on the quantities you give and how often. It is important to give babies a balanced diet, and too much of any one food is undesirable.

Health benefits

Carrots are rich in beta carotene, the antioxidant believed to help fight numerous types of cancers. They are also an excellent source of vitamin A, which helps maintain healthy vision.

Buying and storing

Choose firm, brightly coloured carrots with smooth unblemished skins. Store as for green beans.

Preparation

Wash under cold running water. Young, tender carrots can be scrubbed with a vegetable brush, but older ones will need to be scraped or peeled, then rinsed and sliced.

Cooking

Put carrots in a pan covered with freshly boiled filtered water, bring to the boil, then cover, lower the heat and simmer until tender. Remove from cooking liquid and purée to a smooth texture in a blender. Any remaining cooking liquid can be used to get the right consistency.

Cauliflower (first stage food)

Cauliflower can be introduced once your baby is taking a variety of other vegetables. I find that most young babies prefer it mixed with a little formula or expressed milk or baby rice and served with one or two other vegetables.

Health benefits

Cauliflower is a good source of potassium and vitamin C, and is believed to protect against cancer.

Buying and storing

Choose cauliflowers with creamy white closely packed heads that have no brown spots, and have fresh-looking green leaves. Store as for green beans.

Preparation

Remove the outer green leaves and cut off the woody stem. Break the florets into even-sized pieces and wash well under cold running water.

Cooking

Put florets in a pan and cover with filtered water. Bring to the boil, then lower the heat and simmer, uncovered, until tender. Remove from the heat and purée to a smooth texture in a blender. Any remaining cooking liquid can be used to achieve the right consistency. Alternatively, use a small amount of formula or expressed milk.

Celery (from eight to nine months)

Although some recipe books do introduce celery as a purée, it is not something that I personally have found to be popular with very young babies. I usually introduce it cooked in soups, stews and casseroles from eight months.

Health benefits

Celery is believed to be high in compounds that may help to lower blood pressure and cholesterol levels.

Buying and storing

Choose crisp, light-coloured celery with fresh-looking leaves and blemish-free stalks – the darker green the celery the more stringy it will be. Celery should be stored, loosely wrapped, in the refrigerator and used within one week.

Preparation

Use the inner stalks for babies as they tend to be less tough. Cut off the roots of the stalks and the leaves. Wash well under cold running water, then slice or dice as required.

Cooking

Sauté finely chopped celery and use in stews and soups.

Cheese (between six and seven months)

Because cheese can trigger allergies in some allergic babies it is advisable to start off with very small amounts. It can be used in cooking and is a great finger food.

Health benefits

Cheddar cheese is an excellent source of protein and calcium and is the first cheese to be introduced. Cottage cheese and cream cheese are also high in protein but low in calcium, and some cream cheeses can be very high in salt and should not be given to babies and young children. Choose low-salt varieties. Cheeses such as Camembert and Brie, etc., are not recommended for children under one year of age.

Buying and storing

Choose a mild organic Cheddar cheese that is free from additives and preservatives. Cheese is best wrapped in greaseproof paper to stop it sweating.

Preparation

Finely grate for use in sauces and sandwiches, or cut into sticks.

Cooking

Mild Cheddar cheese can be served in sauces or mixed with vegetarian dishes from six months onwards.

Chicken see Poultry

Courgettes (first stage food)

Courgettes are an ideal first green vegetable to introduce. In my experience very few babies dislike it, especially if it is mixed with sweet potato, baby rice or carrot.

Health benefits
Courgettes are a good source of beta carotene, vitamin C, potassium and folic acid.

Buying and storing
Choose small dark green courgettes with smooth blemish-free skins. Larger courgettes are more likely to have a slightly bitter taste. Store as for green beans.

Preparation
Wash courgettes under cold running water, cut off the ends and slice.

Cooking
Put in a pan and cover with cold filtered water, bring to the boil, then lower the heat and simmer, uncovered until tender. Remove from the cooking liquid and purée to a smooth texture using a blender. Any remaining cooking liquid can be used to achieve the right consistency.

Cucumber (from nine to twelve months)
Once your baby is managing to eat and chew a variety of finger foods well, you can introduce cucumber. Some babies find it more palatable if the skin is removed.

Health benefits
Cucumbers are a source of vitamin C and contain some potassium.

Buying and storing
Choose firm cucumbers with smooth green unblemished skins. Store them in the salad drawer of your refrigerator and use within one week.

Preparation
Wash the cucumber under cold running water, then chop, slice, or

dice into sizes that you think your baby will manage to eat. If you prefer to peel the cucumber, do so just prior to giving it to your baby so that the vitamin C content is not destroyed.

Cooking
Cucumber does not need to be cooked and is best served with salads or dips.

Eggs (from eight to nine months)
Hard-boiled egg yolk can be introduced from eight months, and the hard-boiled white between nine and 12 months. After nine to 12 months, eggs can be scrambled or cooked as an omelette. Soft-boiled eggs should be avoided until your child is one year.

Health benefits
Eggs are an excellent source of vitamin B_{12} and protein and are rich in minerals. The yolks are also a good source of vitamins A and D, but they are high in fat and cholesterol.

Buying and storing
Choose organic free-range eggs and store them in the refrigerator well away from any powerful-smelling foods.

Preparation
Test for freshness just before cooking. Put the egg in a bowl of water; if it floats to the surface it is likely to be old and possibly bad, because the size of the natural air pocket in the egg increases in age. If it stays at the bottom it is fresh.

Cooking
Eggs can be hard-boiled, scrambled or cooked in an omelette.

Figs (from eight to nine months)

Figs are not the most popular food with young babies, but it is worthwhile trying them as they are very nutritious. Once your baby has tasted other dried fruits such as apricots and dates you could try introducing some chopped or puréed figs with breakfast cereal.

Health benefits

Figs are a good source of iron and potassium. Dried figs are also high in fibre, which can prevent constipation.

Buying and storing

There are green, white, purple and black varieties of fig. They have soft, creamy pink flesh full of tiny edible seeds. Most varieties have thin skins, which are edible, though some people prefer to peel figs before eating. Fresh figs should be soft to the touch. They do not keep well, so place in a fruit bowl and eat soon after purchase.

Preparation

Wash half a dozen figs in a colander under cold running water, then leave to soak in a bowl of freshly filtered water overnight.

Cooking

Rinse and put in a pan covered with freshly filtered water. Bring to the boil, cover with a lid, then lower the heat and simmer until the fruit is tender. Remove from the cooking liquid and either purée to a very smooth texture using a blender, or chop into small pieces using a sharp kitchen knife. Serve the figs with your baby's breakfast cereal, yoghurt, rice pudding or custard.

Fish (between six and seven months)

Fish is very nutritious but should be introduced with caution because of the risk of allergies. White fish, such as cod, plaice and haddock, and oily fish, such as salmon and tuna, are equally acceptable. Shellfish can be introduced from 18 months.

Health benefits

Fish is an excellent source of protein and is high in omega-3 fatty acids, which are very healthy for our hearts. Fish is also a good source of vitamin B_{12}. Fish oils and fatty fish are good sources of vitamins A and D.

Buying and storing

Choose fillets of fish that look fresh and moist, have no fishy smell, and are completely free from bones. Fish should be washed under cold running water, then dried with kitchen towel. It should then be placed on a plate which is loosely covered with foil and stored in the coldest part of the refrigerator. All fresh fish should be cooked within 24 hours.

Preparation

Wash a small cod or haddock fillet (approx 50g/2oz) and dry with kitchen towel. Place the fillet in a pan with just enough milk or filtered water to cover it.

Cooking

Bring cooking liquid to the boil, then lower the heat and simmer, uncovered, until tender. Remove the fish from the cooking liquid, check for bones then purée to a smooth texture using a blender. Any remaining cooking liquid can be used to achieve the right consistency. This fish purée should be mixed with a choice of two or three vegetable purées.

Garlic (from nine months)

Garlic can be used in very small amounts from nine months.

Health benefits

Garlic contains a substance that helps fight infections, and may even protect against viruses.

Buying and storing

Choose firm cloves with tight-clinging skin. Store in a cool dry place but not close to other foods as they will absorb the garlic's smell.

Preparation

To peel garlic easily, blanch the cloves in boiling water for about 30 seconds, then drain and cool. Slice off the root. To get the most garlicky taste from garlic cloves, chop or mash them or extract the oil with a garlic press.

Cooking

Garlic should be chopped finely and then lightly fried until soft.

Grapes (from nine to twelve months)

Grapes, like cherries, can be given earlier than nine months as a raw purée. But I usually wait until babies are finger feeding themselves and chewing well, which is usually between nine and 12 months.

Health benefits

Grapes are a good source of potassium. Black grapes are a good source of antioxidants, which help reduce heart disease.

Buying and storing

Choose firm, blemish-free seedless grapes that are still attached to their stems. Grapes are best stored loosely wrapped in the refrigerator and used within 3–4 days.

Preparation

Grapes should be washed just before eating in a colander under cold running water.

Cooking

Put six grapes in a blender and purée to a smooth texture, then press through a sieve to discard the skins. For babies over nine months who are chewing well, grapes can be chopped, mashed or given as halves.

Green beans (first stage food)

French or runner beans are often refused by young babies, so it is important that, like broccoli, the bean purée in the early stages is mixed with enough sweet potato to get your baby gradually used to the taste.

Health benefits

Green beans are a good source of beta carotene, folate, vitamin C and potassium. Some beans are believed to be helpful in regulating blood sugar and cholesterol levels and preventing heart disease.

Buying and storing

Choose small firm crisp green beans, with unblemished, good-coloured skins. Green beans should be stored loosely wrapped in a paper bag in the refrigerator and used within 5–6 days.

Preparation

Wash beans in a colander under cold running water, then top and tail and remove any strings.

Cooking

Put the beans in a pan and just cover with cold filtered water. Bring to the boil then lower the heat and simmer, uncovered, until tender. Remove from the pan and purée to a smooth texture in a blender. Any remaining cooking liquid can be used to achieve the right consistency.

Lamb (from seven to eight months)

If your baby has had no problems digesting chicken, lamb would be the next meat to try. Introducing lamb in casseroles and shepherd's pie is popular with most babies. Note, however, that fatty cuts are high in saturated fats.

Health benefits

Whilst lamb is high in protein and a rich source of most B vitamins, iron, zinc, potassium and phosphorus, it has a higher proportion of saturated fatty acids and more cholesterol than poultry, pork and most beef cuts. Even, lean cuts of lamb should be chosen and trimmed of excess fat.

Buying and storing

Home-produced lamb is at its best in spring, but there is a good supply of imported lamb all year round. Shoulder and leg of lamb are now cut into steaks, and minced lamb is more widely available. When storing, wash, then dry with kitchen towel and store in the fridge loosely wrapped with kitchen foil.

Preparation

Trim off all fat.

Cooking

There are two basic ways of cooking lamb. Less-tender cuts need added liquid and longer, slower cooking, such as braising, pot roasting, stewing and boiling. Tender cuts of meat are best cooked quickly by dry heat – roasting, grilling or dry-frying.

Lentils (between six and seven months)

Red lentils are a favourite with many babies, particularly when used in soups and casseroles. Lentils are classed as an incomplete protein and need to be served with other grains if they are to substitute animal protein as a complete protein. They can cause wind.

Health benefits
Lentils are high in vitamin B$_6$ (pyridoxine), folic acid, iron, potassium, selenium and manganese. They are also a good source of protein and fibre and may be of use to diabetics because they help to regulate blood sugar levels. They lower cholesterol levels, which assists in the fight against heart disease.

Buying and storing
Choose lentils that are well packed, smooth-skinned and evenly coloured. Once opened, lentils are best transferred to an airtight jar or container, where they should keep for up to a year.

Preparation
Lentils, unlike most other pulses, do not need to be soaked, but they should be washed thoroughly in a sieve under cold running water, and any damaged or discoloured ones discarded.

Cooking
Put one tablespoon of lentils into a small pot, add four tablespoons of filtered water and bring to the boil. Cover and simmer until soft and mushy. Remove lentils from cooking liquid and purée to a smooth texture using a blender. Any of the remaining cooking liquid can be used to get the right consistency. Lentils are best served with other vegetable purées such as potato, carrot, leek, etc.

Lettuce (from ten to twelve months)
Although lettuce can be introduced from six months, I would wait until your baby can eat it chopped up in a salad. This may not be until he is about a year old.

Health benefits
The most important nutrients in lettuce are folate and potassium.

Buying and storing
Choose lettuce with fresh bright-looking leaves. Avoid lettuces that show any signs of brown or yellow on the leaves.

Preparation
Never slice, cut or tear lettuce until you are ready to use it. When lettuce cells are torn they release ascorbic acid oxidase, an enzyme which destroys vitamin C.

Liver (from eight to nine months)
Liver can be introduced in small amounts and can be surprisingly popular.

Health benefits
Liver is a very nutritious food for young babies and children. It is high in protein, iron, vitamins A and D, and the B vitamins.

Buying and storing
Choose lamb's liver that is dark-coloured and smells fresh. It should be washed under cold running water and dried with kitchen towel as soon as possible after purchasing. It can then be stored on a plate, loosely covered with foil and stored in the coolest part of the refrigerator. It should be used within two or three days of purchase.

Preparation
Wash under cold running water and dry on kitchen towel.

Cooking
Cut 50g (2oz) of lamb's liver into two pieces. Put in a pan, cover with freshly filtered water and bring to the boil. Cover, lower the heat and simmer until tender. Remove from cooking liquid and purée to a smooth texture in a blender. Any remaining cooking liquid can be used to achieve the right consistency.

Mangoes (first stage foods)

Mango is an excellent food to introduce as a finger food to be eaten raw from six months. Before six months, it is advisable to cook it in a small amount of water to soften it enough. Baby rice served with mango purée is a great favourite with many babies.

Health benefits

Mangoes are a rich source of beta carotene, which the body can convert to vitamin A. They also contain vitamin C.

Buying and storing

Choose ripe mangoes with smooth blemish-free skin that gives slightly when pressed. Ripe mangoes should be stored at a cool temperature or in the refrigerator, where they will keep for 3–4 days.

Preparation

Wash under cold running water, then cut around the middle of the fruit, which should allow you to prise the two sides apart from the stone. Cut the flesh into squares, then turn the fruit inside out. Slice the squares off the skin.

Cooking

Place 10–12 squares in a pan and cover with just enough water to poach them until soft. They can then be mashed with a fork, or puréed in a blender to a smooth texture. Any remaining cooking liquid can be added to achieve the right consistency. From six months onwards, you won't need to cook the mango – simply cut off two or three slices and mash with a fork, or, for babies who are managing finger foods, cut into small bite-sized pieces.

Melon (from seven to eight months)

Melon is an excellent fruit to introduce when your baby is getting used to finger feeding. It is the right texture and needs no cooking.

Health benefits
Some varieties are good sources of beta carotene. Cantaloupe and honeydew melons are good sources of vitamin C.

Buying and storing
Store at room temperature until ripe, thereafter in the refrigerator.

Preparation
Wash the melon under cold running water, cut in half and scoop out the seeds. Cut off as many slices as needed and trim off the skin. The remainder of the melon should be wrapped tightly in foil, stored in the refrigerator and eaten within 1–2 days. The melon that is to be used straight away should either be cut into bite-sized pieces, mashed with a fork, or puréed to a smooth texture in a blender.

Milk (from six months to one year)
Full-fat cow's milk (preferably organic) can be used in small amounts in cooking from the age of six months. It can replace formula or breast milk as a drink once your baby reaches one year. At one year of age your baby will need a minimum of 350ml (12oz) a day, inclusive of milk used in food, sauces, puddings, etc.

Health benefits
Milk is a source of high-quality protein and supplies vitamin A and essential B vitamins together with phosphorus. It is also an excellent source of calcium, which aids the formation of strong bones.

Buying and storing
Until your baby reaches two years of age he needs full-fat cow's milk. Whenever possible, buy organic cow's milk, and ensure that it is sealed when not in use and stored in the refrigerator. Never use milk that is past its sell-by date.

Preparation

By introducing your baby to cow's milk on his cereal and in puddings and sauces he should take to changing from formula or breast milk without any problems. If you do find that he refuses cow's milk to drink, try introducing it a little at a time mixed with formula or expressed breast milk. It can take a couple of weeks, but by increasing the ratio of cow's milk to formula he should reach a stage when he will happily take a full feed of cow's milk.

Cooking

Cow's milk can be used in cooking from six months. However, some nutritionists believe that the introduction of dairy products before one year can trigger allergies in children from allergic families. If you are thinking of avoiding dairy products because of allergy, please consult your GP or dietician.

Mushrooms (from eight to nine months)

In my experience babies either love or hate mushrooms. The best way to serve them is in a sauce or casserole.

Health benefits

Mushrooms are a good source of potassium and vitamin B_2 (riboflavin). They contain almost no fat.

Buying and storing

Choose small cream-coloured button mushrooms with smooth blemish-free skins. Larger flat mushrooms tend to be too strong-tasting for most babies. Store as for asparagus.

Preparation

Wash in a colander under cold running water, prior to cooking.

Cooking

Mushrooms for young babies are best cooked in a sauce or in casseroles.

Oats (from six months)

Oats, including unrefined rolled oatmeal cereal, can be introduced as a breakfast cereal from six months.

Health benefits

Oats contain high quantities of B vitamins and soluble fibre, which can help lower blood cholesterol. They are a good source of carbohydrate or starch, which is the body's main source of energy.

Buying and storing

Choose an unrefined oatmeal cereal that is specifically manufactured for young babies and fortified with extra vitamins and minerals. It should be additive- and gluten-free and have no sugars or fillers such as maltodextrin. Choose organic rolled oats in boxes or packets as opposed to cereal bought in bulk lots, which are much more likely to be exposed to contamination.

Oatmeal should be stored in a cool dry place. Most pre-packed cereals are in airtight boxes to avoid deterioration. If your packet of oatmeal cannot be sealed properly after each use, transfer to an airtight jar or container.

Preparation

Follow the manufacturer's instructions.

Cooking

The majority of first stage baby oatmeal rarely needs cooking. If you choose one that does, follow the manufacturer's instructions.

Parsnips (first stage food)

Parsnips are another vegetable that young babies accept more readily if mixed with one or two other vegetables.

Health benefits

Parsnips are a useful source of beta carotene, folate and vitamin C. They are also high in potassium, phosphorus and iron.

Buying and storing

Choose small firm parsnips with unblemished creamy-coloured skins. Avoid larger parsnips as they are tough. Store as for green beans.

Preparation

Wash under cold running water, peel and slice.

Cooking

Parsnips should be put straight into the pan and covered with freshly filtered water the minute they are prepared to avoid them turning brown. Bring to the boil, cover, then lower the heat and simmer until tender. Remove from cooking liquid and purée to a smooth texture using a blender. Any remaining cooking liquid can be used to achieve the right consistency. Alternatively, formula or expressed milk can be used.

Pasta (between six and seven months)

There is a baby pasta available which does not need puréeing and this is often very popular. Adult pasta is best introduced when finger food is established.

Health benefits

Pasta is high in carbohydrates. These are very important for young babies and children as it provides them with energy.

Buying and storing

Choose organic wholemeal pasta that looks smooth and shiny. Store pasta in airtight containers.

Preparation

The preparation water should be boiling furiously before you add the pasta so that it can penetrate the pasta's starch granules as fast as possible.

Cooking

Pasta should be cooked in fast-boiling filtered water in a large saucepan. Add one tablespoon of oil to the water as this will help prevent the pasta sticking together.

Cooking time depends on the size of the pasta shapes: short pasta pieces will take 6–12 minutes, tiny pasta shapes 2–6 minutes and fresh home-made pasta about 2–4 minutes. Brands do vary enormously in the cooking time required, so always check the packet instructions.

Peaches (first stage food)

Peaches are a great favourite with young babies and can be given before five months as a cooked purée. However, they can be quite fiddly and time-consuming to cook and purée, so I usually introduce them at six months, when they can be given raw.

Health benefits

Peaches are rich in vitamin C and fibre. They may also protect against cancer.

Buying and storing

Choose peaches that are firm to the touch and have a sweet smell. Store at a cool temperature or in the refrigerator where they will keep for 2–4 days.

Preparation

Wash under cold running water, then place in a bowl and cover with boiling water for 1–2 minutes, then straight into a bowl of cold water for 1–2 minutes. This will enable you to peel the peach easily. Cut the fruit into pieces, discarding the stone and pith. For babies over six months old the peach can be cut into bite-sized pieces and given raw.

Cooking

Place the peach in a pan, cover with a little water and poach until tender. Either mash with a fork or purée to a smooth texture using the remainder of the cooking liquid to achieve the right consistency.

Pears (first stage food)

Pear is usually the first fruit that I give to babies as there are very few who dislike it or react badly to it, unlike apple or banana, which can sometimes cause constipation in certain babies when given with baby rice.

Health benefits

Pears are high in natural sugar and are sources of fibre and potassium. The vitamin C in pears is concentrated in the skin.

Buying and storing

Choose Comice pears or pears which are sweet and juicy. It is best to choose fruits that are firm, but slightly under-ripe with unblemished skin. This fruit tends to taste better if it is allowed to ripen in a cool room temperature. Once ripe, they will keep for a further 2–3 days in the refrigerator.

Preparation

Pears, like apples, tend to go brown the minute you peel or cut them. Therefore it is important to cook them as soon as they are prepared. Wash the pear under cold running water, quarter, peel off the skin and remove the core and any pith.

Cooking

Place the pear in a pot with just enough freshly filtered water to cover. Bring the pear and water to the boil, then cover with a lid, lower the heat and simmer until tender. Pears can be inclined to stick when cooking, so keep stirring throughout the cooking. Remove from the pan and either mash with a fork to a very smooth texture or purée in a blender. Any remaining cooking liquid can be used to achieve the right consistency.

From six months, it is not necessary to cook the pear – prepare as above, then mash or grate raw, directly on to food. Once your baby is ready for finger foods, it can be cut into bite-sized pieces.

Peas (first stage food)

The majority of babies love the sweet taste of peas and provided your baby is not prone to bouts of wind, the first stage of weaning is a good time to introduce them in puréed form. Like other green vegetables, peas are best served with another vegetable such as sweet potato, parsnip, etc.

Health benefits

Peas are rich in vitamin B_1 (thiamine) and are a good source of vitamin C. They are a high-protein food and a good source of beta carotene. They may be helpful against heart disease.

Buying and storing

Choose bright green firm, plump unblemished pods – small well-rounded pods usually provide sweeter peas. Peas should be stored loosely wrapped in a brown bag in the refrigerator and used within 2–3 days.

Preparation

Wash the pea pods in a colander under cold running water. Shell the peas into a bowl then wash again in the colander.

Cooking

Put the peas in a pan, bring to the boil, then lower the heat and just cover with freshly boiled filtered water. Bring to the boil, cover, then lower the heat and simmer until the peas are tender. Remove peas from the pan and purée to a very smooth texture, using any of the remaining cooking liquid to adjust the consistency.

Peppers (between six and seven months)

Peppers can be introduced in small amounts to vegetarian dishes and casseroles, and can be served raw in salads from approximately 10 months.

Health benefits

Peppers are rich in vitamin C, which is essential for overall health. They are also a useful source of beta carotene.

Buying and storing

Choose firm brightly coloured peppers with blemish-free skins, that feel thick and fleshy to the touch. Peppers should be stored in the refrigerator to preserve their vitamin content.

Preparation

Wash under cold running water, cut into quarters and remove the seeds and pith, then dice or finely slice according to the recipe.

Cooking

Peppers can be chopped finely and fried before combining with other foods.

Pineapples (from nine to twelve months)

This is popular as a finger food, but can be puréed if your baby finds it difficult to chew.

Health benefits

Pineapples are a good source of vitamin C and manganese.

Buying and storing

Choose large firm blemish-free fruits with fresh-looking green leaves. The pineapple should feel heavy for its size, which is an indicator that it is juicy. Pineapples are best stored at room temperature and eaten when ripe.

Preparation

Wash the pineapple under cold running water, then turn it on its side and cut off the top, then one or two slices. Trim off the skin and cut out the eyes and the core, then cut into bite-sized cubes. For babies whose chewing is not well developed put the pineapple cubes through a blender and purée to a smooth texture. The remainder of the pineapple should be tightly wrapped, stored in the refrigerator and used within a couple of days.

Plums (from seven to eight months)

If your baby is happily digesting a variety of fruits it should be fine to introduce plums at this stage. I have had quite a few babies who have reacted badly to plums and therefore would advise you to introduce very small amounts to begin with.

Health benefits

Plums contain beta carotene and are a good source of potassium. They also contain small amounts of vitamins A, C and B.

Buying and storing

Choose firm but plump, brightly coloured fruits that yield slightly when pressed. Ripe plums should be loosely wrapped in a brown bag, stored in the refrigerator and used within 2–3 days.

Preparation
Wash the plums under cold running water, then place them in a bowl of boiling water for 1–2 minutes. Remove and place in a bowl of cold water until the skins split. Peel off the skin and remove the stones. The fruit can then be puréed to a smooth texture using a fork or a blender. For older babies who have mastered finger foods, they can be chopped into small bite-sized pieces.

Cooking
Place the prepared plums in a pan and cover with freshly filtered water. Bring to the boil and cover, then lower the heat and simmer until tender. Remove from the cooking liquid and purée to a smooth texture using a fork or a blender. Cooked puréed plums are ideal for serving with baby rice, custard or yoghurt.

Potatoes (first stage food)
Potato is high in carbohydrates which are very important for young babies. Sweet potatoes are a particular favourite and an ideal choice to mix with other vegetables, particularly green vegetables.

Health benefits
Potatoes are a good source of vitamin C, potassium and fibre. Most of the vitamin C is found just underneath the skin, so try to cook and serve potatoes with the skins on. They are very high in carbohydrate or starch, and therefore provide lots of energy.

Buying and storing
Choose firm potatoes with blemish-free skin; avoid potatoes that have started to sprout or have green spots on them. Potatoes should ideally be stored in a cool dark airy cupboard to prevent them developing the green spots, which are toxic.

Preparation

Potatoes turn brown very quickly the minute they are cut, so they need to be prepared and cooked immediately. Cooking potatoes in their skins retains more vitamins and avoids this problem. Scrub the potato with a stiff vegetable brush under cold running water.

Cooking

Put in a pan and cover with cold filtered water. Bring to the boil and cover, then lower the heat and simmer until tender. Remove from the cooking liquid and allow the potato to cool slightly before peeling. Potatoes are best mashed to a very fine texture using a fork, then pressed through a sieve. The remainder of the cooking water can be used to adjust the consistency; alternatively, a small amount of formula or breast milk can be used.

Poultry (between six and seven months)

Chicken cooked on its own can be too strong-tasting for some babies. In my experience cooking it in a casserole with vegetables makes it much more palatable for a baby's first taste.

Health benefits

Chicken is usually the first animal protein that babies are given. It is a good source of the B vitamins, protein and iron.

Buying and storing

Oven-ready chickens are sold fresh or frozen, with or without giblets. They range in weight from 1.4 to 3.2kg (3 to 7lb). Pre-basted birds are also available. Corn-fed chicken has a distinctive yellow look and characteristic flavour because it is reared on a diet of maize. Chicken portions are avilable in many forms. In addition to chicken quarters, skinless, boneless breast fillets, thighs and drumsticks, look out for goujons (strips of breast meat). Poultry can contain low levels of salmonella and campylobacter – the bacteria that can cause food poisoning if they multiply, so raw chicken *must* be handled and stored hygienically. Always get poultry home and refrigerate as soon as possible after buying. If the bird contains giblets take them out and store in a separate container.

Preparation

Wash your hands before and after handling and never use the same utensils for preparing raw poultry and cooked food. If you buy frozen poultry, defrost it at cool room temperature rather than the fridge. Frozen food must be fully thawed before cooking.

Cooking

Always ensure poultry is cooked thoroughly. To test, pierce the thickest part of the thigh with a skewer. Only when the juices run clear – not at all pink – is the poultry cooked. Put leftover cooked poultry in the fridge as soon as it's cold and eat within two days.

Prunes (from eight to nine months)

These are best given when your baby is established on finger foods.

Health benefits

Prunes are a good source of the B vitamins and of potassium and iron. They are a useful source of fibre and can relieve constipation.

Buying and storing

Some varieties are tenderised and do not need soaking, otherwise soak in filtered water or fruit juice. Store dried prunes in an airtight container.

Preparation

Most dried fruits need washing and soaking for at least three hours or overnight. However, some do not require soaking and come vacuum-packed and ready to eat. These can be kept sealed in the bag for future use.

Pulses (from seven to eight months)

Pulses, or dried beans, are an excellent form of vegetable protein but need to be served with another whole grain such as brown rice, wholewheat pasta, wholemeal bread, etc., if they are to replace a serving of animal protein. Apart from red lentils and butter beans, I have found that the majority of other pulses and dried beans are too difficult for young babies to digest and can cause wind. By seven months the majority of babies are established on three solid meals a day and should then be able to digest beans and pulses.

Health benefits

Beans are rich in carbohydrate and are a good source of protein and fibre. They are low in fat and contain B vitamins and folic acid. They can help control blood sugar and lower cholesterol levels.

Buying and storing

Choose smooth-skinned, uniformly sized, evenly coloured beans that are free of stones and debris. Check the use-by date on the packet. Beans over one year old become tough and lose their flavour. Avoid beans sold in bulk as they may have been exposed to air and light and may have insect contamination (tiny holes in the bean indicate that an insect has burrowed into or through the bean). Store beans in airtight containers.

Preparation

Wash dried beans and pick them over carefully, discarding any damaged or withered beans and any that float. (Only withered beans are light enough to float in water.)

Cover the beans with filtered water, bring to the boil, and then set them aside to soak for 24 hours. When you are ready to use the beans, discard the water in which they have been soaked. Some of the indigestible sugars in the beans will leach out into the water, making them less gassy.

Cooking

Beans are best used in soups and stews.

Pumpkin (between six and seven months)

Pumpkin soup is often a great favourite with babies.

Health benefits

Pumpkins are a good source of beta carotene and a useful source of vitamin E.

Buying and storing

Choose a pumpkin with bright orange blemish-free skin. You can also buy slices of pumpkin sold by weight.

Preparation

Cut the pumpkin in half and scoop out the seeds. Cut into sections and peel and chop the flesh into even-sized pieces.

Cooking

Cook the pumpkin in boiling filtered water for about 15 minutes, or steam. Drain well and mash.

Spinach (from seven to eight months)

Introduce spinach with caution as some babies can have mild reactions. However, it is a vegetable that can be used in many meals.

Health benefits

Spinach is an excellent source of beta carotene and a good source of vitamin C, which may help prevent cancer. It is also a good source of potassium and folic acid. While spinach has a high content of iron, the oxalic acid in the leaves renders it unavailable.

Buying and storing

Choose fresh-looking spinach with dark-green blemish-free leaves. Store loosely wrapped in the refrigerator and use within two days.

Preparation

Wash the spinach leaves in filtered water several times as it collects dirt.

Cooking

Summer spinach should be steamed for 3–4 minutes in just the water that clings to the leaves. Winter spinach needs to have the stalks and central ribs removed before boiling in filtered water. Cook covered for 5–10 minutes in a large saucepan. Drain well and press with the back of a wooden spoon. Serve either puréed or roughly chopped.

Swede and turnip (first stage food)

Swede and turnip are ideal for mixing with other vegetables at the outset of weaning. They both go particularly well with potato and carrots.

Health benefits

Swede and turnip are good sources of vitamin C, beta carotene and fibre.

Buying and storing

Choose firm, well-formed small-to-medium swedes and turnips with blemish-free skins. Like potatoes, they are best stored unwashed in a cool dark airy cupboard where they will keep for up to two months. Stored at room temperature they would need to be used within a week.

Preparation

Scrub the swede or turnip under cold running water and cut off one or two slices approximately 1.25cm (½in) thick. Peel the skin off, then cut into cubes.

Cooking

Place the swede or turnip in a pan just covered with freshly filtered water. Bring to the boil, cover, then lower the heat and simmer until tender. Remove from the cooking liquid and purée to a smooth texture using a blender. Any remaining cooking liquid can be used to adjust the purée to the right consistency.

Tomatoes (from seven to eight months)

Health benefits

Tomatoes are medium in sugar but have no starch. They are an excellent source of vitamin C and a good source of potassium. They are best served fresh and ripe.

Buying and storing

Choose smooth, round or oval tomatoes. The tomatoes should feel heavy for their size; their flesh should be firm, not watery. If you plan to use them immediately, pick ripe ones whose skin is a deep orange/red colour. If you plan to store the tomatoes for a few days, pick tomatoes whose skin is still slightly yellow or pink. Avoid bruised tomatoes or tomatoes with mould around the stem end. The damaged tomatoes may be rotten inside; the mouldy ones may be contaminated with mycotoxins (poisons produced by moulds).

Preparation

Remove and discard all the stalks and leaves – they are poisonous. Wash the tomatoes under cool running water, then slice and serve. Alternatively, peel the tomatoes by plunging them into boiling water, then transferring them on a slotted spoon into a bowl of cold water. The change in temperature damages a layer of cells just under the skin so that the skins slip off easily. To get rid of the seeds, cut the tomato in half across the middle and squeeze the two halves gently, cut side down, over a bowl. The seeds should pop out easily.

Vegetable oils (from seven to eight months)
Health benefits
Vegetable oils are our best source of vitamin E. Best used only once and certainly not after repeated use in a chip fryer.

Buying and storing
Choose tightly sealed bottles of vegetable oil, protected from light and heat.

Yoghurt (between six and seven months)
Health benefits
Yoghurt, like all milk products, is a good source of thiamine (vitamin B_1) and riboflavin (vitamin B_2). It is also a good source of calcium.

Buying and storing
Choose tightly sealed, refrigerated containers. Check the date on the container to buy the freshest product.

Preparation
Do not 'whip' yoghurt before adding it to any dish; you will break the curd and make the yoghurt watery.

Useful addresses

Baby equipment
The Great Little Trading Company
Pondwood Close
Moulton Park
Northampton NN3 6DF
Tel: 0870 850 6000

Cooking equipment
Little plastic pots, containers for freezing meals in bulk as well as a range of food processors are available from all John Lewis Partnership stores throughout the UK.

Suppliers of organic produce
The Soil Association provides information about deliveries of organic vegetables in your area.
Tel: 01179 290 661
To order their full organic shopping catalogue:
Tel: 01179 142 446

The Fresh Food Company offers a home delivery service of organic vegetables, meat, fish, game, dairy produce and bread nationwide.
Tel: 020 8969 0351

Visit Gina Ford's website: www.contentedbaby.com

Further reading

The Contented Child's Food Bible by Gina Ford & Paul Sacher (Vermilion, 2004)

The Contented Toddler Years by Gina Ford (Vermilion, 2006)

The Food Our Children Eat by Joanna Blythman (Fourth Estate, 1999)

The Gina Ford Baby and Toddler Cook Book by Gina Ford (Vermilion, 2005)

Good First Foods by Sara Lewis (Hamlyn, 2002)

The New Contented Little Baby Book by Gina Ford (Vermilion, 2006)

Optimum Nutrition for Babies & Young Children by Lucy Burney (Piatkus, 1999)

Planet Organic: Baby & Toddler Cookbook by Lizzie Vann (Dorling Kindersley, 2000)

What to Expect When You're Breast-feeding . . . And What if You Can't? by Clare Byam-Cook (Vermilion, 2006)

Index

Also by Gina Ford
Available from Vermilion

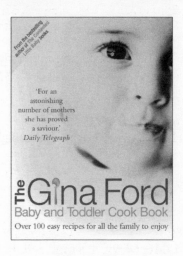

Picking up where *The Contented Little Baby Book of Weaning* leaves off, *The Gina Ford Baby and Toddler Cook Book* addresses the next stage in childhood nutrition. Packed with nutritional advice and delicious recipes, its unique family-centred approach shows how it's possible for babies and their parents to enjoy the same meals together.

With over 150 recipes from classics like Shepherd's Pie to more unusual ideas such as Fruity Lamb Tagine and Gina's very own Bubble and Squeak Potato cakes, all the recipes in this book are quick and easy to prepare. In her inimitable style, Gina also suggests clever time-saving devices to help fit good wholesome cooking into a busy family life; from adapting a single recipe to suit every family member through to batch cooking, and from creative use of leftovers through to quick finger foods.

The Gina Ford Baby and Toddler Cook Book is the perfect one-stop-guide for parents who want to feed their children delicious and healthy food and make family mealtimes a treat for everyone.

'With glossy pictures of happy, well-fed children and tasty recipes, this is an impressive package . . . It's all very yummy stuff' Junior

The prospect of bringing a tiny baby home for the first time is daunting. Take heart because *The New Contented Little Baby Book* is here to help you.

Fully updated and including helpful input from clients, readers and mothers who love her routines, *The New Contented Little Baby Book* gives you reassuring and practical advice from Britain's number one childcare expert, Gina Ford.

Gina's secret is simple and the results are amazing. She has devised a strategy that is easy to follow and is understanding of the needs of individual babies. Once you've established her routines, everything else will follow: you'll have a contented little baby *and* be a calm and contented parent too!

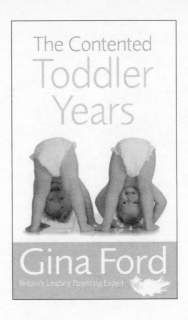

The Contented
Toddler
Years

Gina Ford
Britain's Leading Parenting Expert

In *The New Contented Little Baby Book*, Gina Ford guides parents through their baby's first year. But as a baby grows, so his or her routines and patterns change. In *The Contented Toddler Years* Gina addresses the demands and needs of your growing toddler. From walking and talking, to teething and potty training, Gina offers her invaluable down-to-earth advice and insight into these crucial stages of your child's development.

The
Complete
Sleep Guide

for Contented Babies
and Toddlers

Gina Ford

Britain's Leading Parenting Expert

Sleep is one of the most misunderstood and confusing aspects of
parenthood. While many babies fall naturally into a good sleeping
pattern, latest research shows that the majority do not, leading to
months, and sometimes years, of stressful, sleepless nights for children
and parents. If your child has trouble sleeping or you simply wish to
avoid sleep problems for your new baby now, and as it grows older,
Gina Ford's practical step-by-step guide is the one for you.

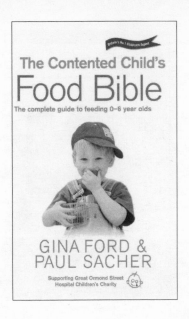

The Contented Child's
Food Bible
The complete guide to feeding 0–6 year olds

GINA FORD &
PAUL SACHER

Supporting Great Ormond Street
Hospital Children's Charity

Feeding your child can be one of the hardest aspects of parenting; there is now clear evidence stating that what children eat can affect their future physical and intellectual development. The media is full of information on nutrition and diet but knowing what to apply to your own child can be difficult. In *The Contented Child's Food Bible*, Gina Ford and Paul Sacher, a specialist dietitian at Great Ormond Street Hospital, offer practical and down-to-earth advice for parents struggling with the many difficulties of feeding; ranging from the benefits of breast-feeding to overcoming snacking and getting your child to eat fruit and vegetables every day. They also provide the latest information about what kinds of food children need for good growth, health and development. This accessible guide is the one you need to establish healthy eating habits for your child for life.

Gina Ford knows from experience that one area of parenting that can be a big, scary hurdle for parents is potty training. The good news is that it's very easy when you know all the tips and tricks and there is no need for tantrums or endless hours spent sitting with a toddler who refuses to go potty.

With handy tips and anecdotes from parents who have been there, including advice on accidents, rewards and bed-wetting, *Potty Training in One Week* will help you do just that – and you won't have to tear your hair out in the process.

Gina Ford's Top Tips for
Contented
Babies &
Toddlers

Gina Ford
Britain's Leading Parenting Expert

Britain's leading childcare expert offers you her top tips for guaranteeing happy, healthy little babies . . .

Gina Ford guides you through the key stages of baby and toddler care including sleeping, weaning, feeding, potty training and behavioural development with her invaluable, sound and practical advice on parenting. This handy guide will fit in your handbag to make it quick and easy to access, wherever you are.